MIGHTY ROBOTS

Mechanical Marvels that Fascinate and Frighten

BY
DAVID
JONES

ANNICK PRESS

TORONTO • NEW YORK • VANCOUVER

Annick Press Ltd.

We acknowledge the support of the Canada Council for the Arts, the Ontario Arts Council, and the Government of Canada through the Book Publishing Industry Development Program (BPIDP) for our publishing activities.

Edited by Pam Robertson
Copy edited by John Sweet; photo research by John Sweet
Proofread by Elizabeth McLean
Cover and interior design by Irvin Cheung/iCheung Design
Front cover photo of Cog © Sam Ogden
Front cover photo of Pearl reproduced courtesy of Carnegie Mellon University

Special thanks to Dr. Robot for images used at the end of each chapter. www.drrobot.com

The text was typeset in Apollo, Eurostile & Citizen

Cataloging in Publication
Jones, David (David Richard), 1956-
Mighty robots : mechanical marvels that fascinate and frighten / by
David Jones.

Includes index.
ISBN 1-55037-929-1 (bound).—ISBN 1-55037-928-3 (pbk.)

1. Robots—Juvenile literature. I. Title.

TJ211.2.J66 2005   629.8'92   C2005-901462-8

Printed and bound in China

Published in the U.S.A. by
Annick Press (U.S.) Ltd.

Distributed in Canada by
Firefly Books Ltd.
66 Leek Crescent
Richmond Hill, ON
L4B 1H1

Distributed in the U.S.A. by
Firefly Books (U.S.) Inc.
P.O. Box 1338
Ellicott Station
Buffalo, NY 14205

Visit our website at: **www.annickpress.com**

Contents

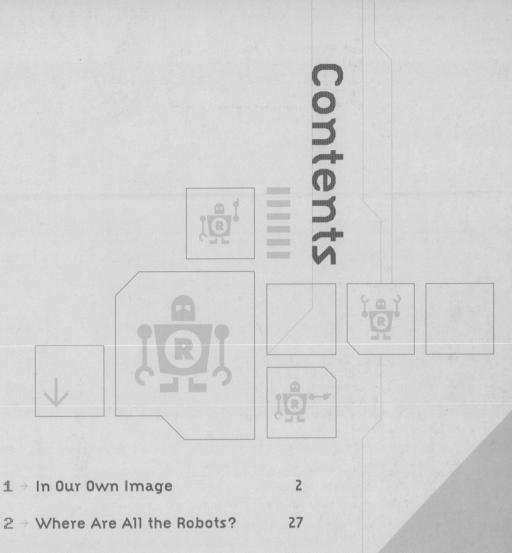

chapter 1

In Our Own Image

What do you see when you hear the word *robot*? A mechanical arm in a darkened factory, welding a car body in a veil of sparks? Or maybe you picture a tractor rolling over a sand dune on Mars, pausing to collect a scoop of rust-colored dirt. Or a tiny submarine drifting through the corridors of a sunken ship.

All of these machines are real robots. And yet it's far more likely that you envisioned something in the form of a man, perhaps clanking out of the dark with glowing eyes, reaching for you with metal claws. The robots we have seen in movies and read about in stories live in our imaginations. They are what we think

of when we hear the word *robot*. For a century now, we've had a recurring dream of a mechanical man—a servant to obey our every command. Such a machine would free us of all our dull labors. While it's taking out the garbage or walking the dog, we could go to the beach or see a movie.

But for every dream, there is a nightmare. Robots also frighten us. The metal bodies that make them powerful servants give them the strength to crush us. We ask, "Will a machine created in our image look favorably upon us, its creator?" Since we began imagining robots, our answer has almost always been no.

Although we may one day succeed in building a machine in our own image, we probably won't be able to predict what it will do. Like people, such a machine will act independently—maybe even against our wishes. Perhaps that is why robots both fascinate and frighten us.

What Exactly Is a Robot?

While the idea of the robot began as a machine in the form of a human being, few real robots look anything like us. They toil away in factories, the depths of the ocean, or outer space, far from human eyes. We send them to places where people cannot, or would rather not, go.

Most robots are machines that replace human effort, built to do something that otherwise a person would have to do. Some robots are toys, but most are labor-saving devices.

A dishwasher is a labor-saving device. Does that make it a robot? No. A dishwasher is an automatic machine; it does the same thing over and over. So is a conveyor belt in an auto factory. All it does is move forward, carrying a product or a part to the next worker. But a robot welder can be reprogrammed to move to any position within its reach before welding two parts together, depending on what it is making.

There is a second kind of robot that does only what people tell it—usually using a joystick or other form of remote control. It's called a *telerobot*. While a telerobot might surprise a stranger, its actions are entirely predictable to its operator. It has no capacity for independent behavior. For this reason, some people don't consider telerobots to be true robots.

And yet telerobots are the most successful robots of all. We send them into places that are too dangerous, small, or unpleasant for people. There are telerobots that put out fires, explore sunken ships, or peer across the universe and back through time. In fact, almost all the robots working outside of factories are telerobots. Because they have proven so useful, telerobots are included in this book.

True robots change their behavior by sensing the world around them, then acting on this information. They may be able to hear a human voice and move towards it, or recognize one object in a bin full of different things and pick it up. But such robots are rare. Only now are they starting to make their way into our homes.

Today, almost all robots are at least partly controlled by computers. So does that make your home computer a robot? Not really. Your computer can't move. Whether a robot looks like a human being or not, or is controlled by a joystick or a software program, all or part of its body moves.

The dream of roboticists (scientists who build and study robots) has long been to make a machine capable of doing what a person can. Such a machine would have to be intelligent.

But what do we mean by "intelligent"? There are many definitions of the word. One that would be applicable to robots is "having the ability to apply knowledge to manipulate one's environment." Another one is "having the ability to deal with new or trying situations."

Alan Turing is considered to be the father of the branch of study known as artificial intelligence, or AI. Turing was part of the team of scientists who built Enigma, a machine that allowed the Allies to decipher coded messages sent by the Germans during World War II. Most historians acknowledge that without Enigma, the Allies would never have won the war.

Shortly after the war, Turing gave the first public lecture on artificial intelligence. "What we want," he said, "is a machine that can learn from experience." He added that such a machine would have the ability to alter its own instructions.

The History of the Robot

Many have called Mary Shelley's novel *Frankenstein* the world's first work of science fiction. In the story, written in 1816, Victor Frankenstein sews together a manlike creature using various body parts taken from dead people. He brings his creature to life with an electric charge furnished by a bolt of lightning. Shortly after he succeeds in bringing his brainchild to life, Frankenstein gives it a series of lessons to help it function in the world.

Although he was assembling organs and limbs rather than wires and motors, Frankenstein's goal was very much the same as that stated by Alan Turing over a century later: to create an artificial being able to learn from experience. So, had he been a real person, would Frankenstein have qualified as the world's first roboticist?

Maybe. But to trace the origins of the robot we have to go back way before the good doctor began robbing the local graveyards. People have been trying to create machines in the forms of animals and people for thousands of years.

The plans for this automaton were drawn up by Hero of Alexandria, who lived in ancient Greece. If the human figure holding the club were turned to one side, a valve in the pedestal opened, allowing water to flow from one chamber to another. The resulting vacuum would cause the dragon to sip water from a bowl held up to its mouth.

Automatons

Much of the technology used in early robots was developed in toys called *automatons*. These toys were often very delicate and expensive, and so they were usually owned by adults and not children. Most of them were figures in the shapes of people or animals. They could be powered by springs, weights, or hand-turned cranks.

Hero of Alexandria, a mathematician and inventor who lived around 62 CE, drew up simple plans for figures that played musical instruments, birds that chirped, or hunters who shot arrows at dragons. No one knows if he ever actually constructed any of these automatons; if he did, only the plans survived. Most of the automatons seem beyond the technology of Hero's time, but they are some of the earliest known designs to make use of *hydraulics* and *pneumatics*—the techniques of powering machines by forcing liquids or air through pipes and hoses.

Today, the movements of the animatronic figures you see in theme parks like Disneyland are still powered mainly by hydraulic or pneumatic devices. Pneumatic (air-driven) mechanisms have largely replaced hydraulic (oil- or water-driven) machines because pneumatics are much faster and lighter, if not as powerful or smooth as hydraulics. Also, if an air hose

←

Two Chahakobi Ningyos, or tea-serving dolls. The doll on the right has had its head and clothing removed to show the workings inside. It was a fairly simple design, but impressive considering that it was made almost entirely of wood. Much of the mechanism was based on technology developed by 17th-century Japanese clockmakers.

puppets called Karakuri. The most common was a doll that served tea. When a cup was set on a tray the doll carried, the doll shuffled forward. When the cup was removed, it triggered a switch that caused the doll to turn and walk back the way it came. (Actually, the doll rolled on wheels, but a pair of wooden feet dangling beneath the hem of its dress made it appear to walk.) These dolls were powered by springs made of baleen, the bone-like material that whales use to strain plankton from the water.

Although automatons did have the power of independent movement, they weren't robots because they could only perform the same actions over and over. That changed when a man named Jacques de Vaucanson built the first programmable automaton, nearly 300 years ago.

leaks a little during a show, it doesn't matter too much. If a hydraulic arm full of oil leaks, the results can be quite memorable. Crowds visiting the Hall of Presidents exhibit at Disneyland will probably never forget seeing Abe Lincoln—apparently too patriotic to excuse himself from the proceedings for even a moment—wet his pants.

In the 1600s, the Japanese built

The First Robots

Jacques de Vaucanson was born in Grenoble, France, in 1709, the son of a master glove maker. He was interested in mechanical devices from an early age, and built his first clock just from observing one in the church where his mother went to confession.

When Jacques was only seven, his father died and Jacques was sent away to a monastery to study. The math teacher there soon recognized his talent and helped him in his studies.

After leaving college, de Vaucanson fell ill and lay in bed for four months. During that time he had a fever and dreamed of an *android* (a robot resembling a man) that could play the flute. When he recovered, he began making elaborate drawings. He had craftsmen make the pieces, then assembled the flute player himself. It was the size of an adult musician and could play 12 different songs.

The remarkable thing about the flute player was that it didn't just *appear* to play the flute, it really did. The musician, made mostly of wood and cardboard, blew into the mouthpiece and played different notes by moving its fingers to open and close holes on an ordinary flute, just as a human flute player does. The fingers and lips had leather tips so that they could better seal the holes. There was nothing special about the flute; if it were replaced by any other standard-sized flute, the automaton would still work.

The flute player's breath was supplied by nine bellows connected to the mouth by pipes, and the lips and a metal tongue regulated the speed and force of the air. A wooden cylinder with little pegs sticking from its surface controlled the player's movements. The automaton could be "reprogrammed" to play a different song by changing the cylinder. The whole thing was powered by a series of weights and pulleys, just as the clocks of that time were.

It took de Vaucanson four years to finish the flute player, after which he put it on display in a hotel in Paris, where thousands of people came to watch it. The price of admission was very high—a week's wages for a manual laborer. Still, the show was a great success.

De Vaucanson went on to build a tambourine player and then perhaps his greatest automaton, a duck. Like the flute player, the duck's movements were driven by weights and gears hidden in the pedestal on which the duck stood. The power was transmitted by pulleys passing through the duck's legs.

The duck could flap its wings, squat or stand, and move its neck from side to side. But its most impressive trick was its ability to dabble. Presented with a bowl of water with some corn floating in it, it could pick up a kernel with its bill, tilt its head back, and swallow it. Every so often it would poop out a small green pellet.

De Vaucanson quickly grew bored with his automatons, but they brought him such fame that in 1741 he was appointed to the position of inspector of the manufacture of silk in France—a very important industry. At the time, weavers in France were losing work to their competitors in England and Scotland, and de Vaucanson was charged with reforming the country's silk manufacturing process. He decided that the best way to improve the industry was to automate it, that is, turn as much of the manufacturing process as possible over to machines.

Looms, the machines that weavers used to make cloth, were already semi-automated. As with the duck and the flute player, the actions of early automated looms were controlled by pegged cylinders. Later, loops of paper dotted with patterns of holes replaced the cylinders. These were followed by flat cards very much like the punch cards that would control electronic computers 200 years later.

De Vaucanson added a ratcheting mechanism to advance these cards automatically. Now the weaver had only to power the loom; the punch cards controlled all of its motions. The actions of the loom controlled the pattern on the cloth it produced. As long as the pattern of holes on the punch card was correct, the loom turned out cloth without any errors in the weave and it did it far more quickly than a weaver working with a couple of assistants. These assistants were among the first people to lose their jobs to machines.

Not surprisingly, de Vaucanson was anything but a hero to France's silk workers. They pelted him with stones in the streets, and the inventor was forced to go into hiding. It wasn't until Joseph Marie Jacquard found a working model of de Vaucanson's loom in a museum in Paris in 1803—years after the inventor had died—and added some of its features to his own design that it was put into widespread use.

Some have called de Vaucanson's loom the world's first industrial robot, even if it was powered by a human being. Others reserve that honor for later inventors, such as the Englishman Edmund Cartwright, who completed the automation process by inventing a steam-powered loom in 1785. This was indisputably an early factory robot: it was programmable, it moved, and it eventually replaced human workers by the tens of thousands—though not before they burned down the factory in which it was first installed.

For a century after the invention of the programmable automaton, there was very little progress in robotic technology. But during this period a curious thing happened: the *idea* of the robot began to advance beyond the science. People began writing stories about mechanical men that could do the work of people—just as they were writing stories about ships that could travel through space or time. The robot became a staple of science fiction.

One of the earliest of these stories was *The Steam Man of the Prairies*, which first appeared in Irwin's American Novels in 1865. The author of *The Steam Man* was Edward S. Ellis, a teacher turned writer who wrote hundreds of books under many different names.

The steam man was not a true robot. It had no will of its own or ability to make decisions, and was essentially a locomotive in the form of a man. It walked or ran from place to place, usually pulling a rather ordinary cart carrying its inventor, Johnny Brainerd. Brainerd was a teenaged dwarf, and a genius.

[The steam man] was about ten feet in height, measuring to the top of the "stove-pipe hat," which was fashioned after the common order of felt coverings, with a broad brim, all painted a shiny black. The face was made of iron, painted a black color, with a pair of fearful eyes, and a tremendous grinning mouth. A whistle-like contrivance was trade to answer for the nose. The steam chest proper and boiler were where the chest in a human being is generally supposed to be, extending also into a large knapsack arrangement over the shoulders and back . . .

In the knapsack were the valves, by which the steam or water was examined. In front was a painted imitation of a vest, in which a door opened to receive the fuel, which, together with the water, was carried in the wagon, a pipe running along the shaft and connecting with the boiler.

While the steam man was beyond the technology of its time, the idea must have seemed believable to readers. For over a century, steam power had been replacing animals and gravity in all kinds of jobs, from pumping water out of mines to propelling carriages and locomotives.

It was a full 20 years before the robot in *The Steam Man* was replaced by a more advanced, electric model, the subject of another series of novels. The

The Tin Man from *The Wizard of Oz* is not actually a robot, but a cyborg—a hybrid of a machine and a living organism. He began as a human woodcutter, but in a series of accidents managed—somehow—to cut off his own legs and arms. As each limb was lost, it was replaced with a mechanical equivalent.

· THE TIN MAN ·

electric man looked a little like a medieval suit of armor and also pulled a cart, this one carrying the generator needed to power the robot. It traveled all over the world, defeating entire armies and fighting the hordes of jungle natives who were always throwing spears or shooting arrows at it. Like the steam man, its adventures were followed by thousands of readers in the United States.

The next robots to appear in literature were probably the Tin Woodman and Tic-Tok—a mechanical man powered by clock-works. Both of these robots were characters in the hugely popular Oz books written by L. Frank Baum and published starting in 1900. The Tin Woodman was the first of a type that would pop up again and again in fiction over the next century: the robot who yearns to become human. He believed that he had only to acquire a heart in order to love.

Karel Capek and Rossum's Universal Robots

While Ellis and later writers dreamed of mechanical men, at this point nobody had ever used the word *robot*—at least not in the way we use it today. It was not until a Czech playwright, Karel Capek, wrote a play in 1920 that the word was first used to refer to an artificial human being. He borrowed the term from the old Czech word *robota*, meaning "forced labor."

The play was *R.U.R.*, which stands for Rossum's Universal Robots. It's the story of an idealistic young woman, Helena Glory, who travels to a remote island where a factory turns out robots designed to replace human factory workers. Like people, they are made of flesh and blood, but they are produced from vats of chemicals.

In the play, the original inventors of these robots were father and son. The elder Rossum had hoped to create a robot that was human in every way. His son was more interested in creating a worker without a soul, desires, or imagination—in other words, a superior factory employee.

The younger Rossum wins out, and the island factory becomes very profitable. But Helena convinces a scientist at the factory to create robots using Rossum senior's formula. She hopes to give these more human robots souls and eventually free them from their life of drudgery.

The plan goes terribly wrong

11

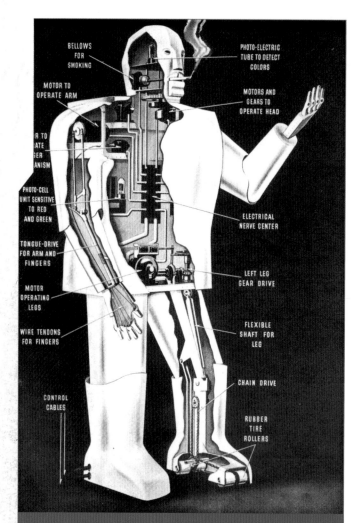

BELLOWS FOR SMOKING

PHOTO-ELECTRIC TUBE TO DETECT COLORS

MOTOR TO OPERATE ARM

MOTORS AND GEARS TO OPERATE HEAD

R TO
ATE
GER
ANISM

PHOTO-CELL UNIT SENSITIVE TO RED AND GREEN

ELECTRICAL NERVE CENTER

TONGUE-DRIVE FOR ARM AND FINGERS

MOTOR OPERATING LEGS

LEFT LEG GEAR DRIVE

WIRE TENDONS FOR FINGERS

FLEXIBLE SHAFT FOR LEG

CONTROL CABLES

CHAIN DRIVE

RUBBER TIRE ROLLERS

Elektro was built by the Westinghouse Corporation as a robotic ambassador to the 1939 World's Fair in New York. Along with its mechanical dog, Sparko, Elektro greeted visitors to the Westinghouse pavilion, and proved to be one of the fair's most popular attractions. Under the control of a nearby operator, the automaton could roll along on its feet, speak, move its arms and fingers, and—essential for life in the 1930s—smoke cigarettes.

when the newly aware robots come to view their human inventors as impediments to order and productivity. At the play's climax, they swarm onto the stage, killing anyone they can find.

R.U.R. was a hit. A few years after its debut in Prague, it was translated into English and performed all over the world. Although Karel's brother Josef (also a writer) first coined the word *robot*, in a letter to Karel, it was Karel's play that brought the term into common use. Today, science-fiction writers are more likely to use the word *android* for a robot that closely resembles a human being, while *robot* is now associated with workers that are obviously mechanical.

A few years after *R.U.R.* burst upon the stage, the first robot ever to appear onscreen debuted in the movie *Metropolis*. The evil Maria was created by a scientist to discredit a human character of the same name, and could move and talk as well as her double. Maria was followed about a decade later by the Annihilants, robotic soldiers of Ming the Merciless, the evil villain of the Flash Gordon films.

The idea of machines that could function as well as human beings was becoming fixed in people's minds. So too was the idea of machines that could turn against their makers.

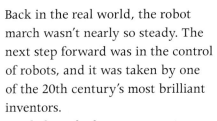

Back in the real world, the robot march wasn't nearly so steady. The next step forward was in the control of robots, and it was taken by one of the 20th century's most brilliant inventors.

Nikola Tesla, born in 1856, is famed for inventing radio and alternating current (the type of electrical current we use in our homes). He also invented speedometers, electrical generators, and even a method of transmitting electrical power from place to place without wires. And he had plans for hundreds of other inventions, including a ring around the equator supported on scaffolding. Once completed, the scaffolding would be removed and—voilà—the ring would float in place. If the ring were set rolling, Tesla reasoned, it could be used as a moving highway. All one would have to do is get on or off. Tesla never managed to iron out all the details of that project—like finding a material strong enough to make such a structure.

On a more practical level, Tesla actually built and demonstrated the world's first remote-controlled robot—a small boat. It was about the size and shape of an old-fashioned bathtub. At one end were a rudder and a propeller. Inside the tub were several motors to drive the rudder and propeller, as well as batteries to power the motors.

Tesla's most important contribution to robotics was the boat's *coherers*, the world's first radio-activated switches. These were essentially small canisters filled with metallic-oxide powders. When radio waves from Tesla's remote control passed through the canister, the powder would align itself along the lines of the magnetic field created by the radio waves. The powder then became conductive, allowing an electrical current to pass through it. These switches controlled the boat's rudder, propeller, and running lights.

At the time, nobody was using radio waves for communication, but Tesla had been experimenting with them for several years, sending and receiving signals over distances of up to 50 kilometers (30 miles). Tesla thought that his robotic boat would be an ideal way to demonstrate a practical use for radio waves. In 1898, he had a large tank filled with water in Madison Square Garden in New York City. There, he showed his boat to a crowd of scientists, the general public, and representatives from the U.S. Navy.

A reporter suggested that the boat could be filled with explosives and used as a weapon. Tesla bristled,

13

If the automated loom was the first factory robot, Willard Pollard Jr. and Harold Roselund's robotic arm was the second. The arm, powered by electric motors, was designed to spray paint in a programmed pattern. It was based on a very old mechanism called a *pantograph*. To see one in action, look at the arm that controls the angle of the rear derailleur on most bicycles. That's a pantograph. So are most modern car jacks. It's like two pairs of scissors riveted together at the blade tips. Opening or closing one pair causes the second pair to move in the same way.

In Pollard and Roselund's design, electric motors at the base of the pantograph controlled the far end, where a spray gun was attached. Even though it was built over 150 years after the steam-powered loom, the movement of the pantograph was controlled in the same way—by a strip of film with holes punched in it. The frequency of the holes controlled the speeds of the electric motors.

Although the inventors applied for a patent in 1934, the robotic arm wasn't built for another six years. The design was never widely used, but it introduced the idea of a machine that could position a tool—any tool—precisely in space. Such arms eventually proved to be the key to automating modern factories.

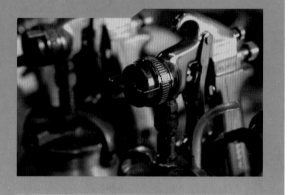

"You do not see there a wireless torpedo, you see there the first of a race of robots, mechanical men which will do the laborious work of the human race!"

Tesla called his invention a *tele-automaton*, and it was indeed the world's first tele-operated robot. As impressive as the demonstration was, however, the military showed no interest in funding Tesla's plans for developing a fleet of remote-controlled boats. Almost 20 years later the navy financed some trials of a similar vessel, but by then Tesla's patents on the device had expired. The money went to someone else.

Tesla died in 1943 without a penny to his name, despite inventions that went on to become the pillars of the world's economy. It was not until the year of his death that the United States Supreme Court recognized Tesla, and not Marconi, as the true inventor of radio.

Asimov and the Laws of Robotics

By now, the mechanical monsters were running rampant through the pages of science-fiction magazines such as *Amazing Stories* and *Astounding Science Fiction*. The covers frequently featured robots, usually carrying swooning maidens back to the lairs of their fiendish inventors or grinding tanks under their iron heels.

In contrast, the stories between these covers were often thoughtful. One author who took robots very seriously was Isaac Asimov, one of the most prolific and successful of all science-fiction writers. Asimov asked himself a question: were there a few simple rules that, if obeyed, could keep robots from becoming poster boys for *Weird Tales*? In answer, he came up with his laws of robotics—three unbreakable rules that were programmed into the brain of each of his fictional robots.

1) A robot may not injure a human being or, through inaction, allow a human being to come to harm.

2) A robot must obey the orders given to it by human beings, except where such orders would conflict with the First Law.

3) A robot must protect its own existence as long as such protection does not conflict with the First or Second Law.

The laws were clearly designed to protect people first and their mechanical servants second.

In 1942, Asimov introduced his three laws to the world in a short story called "Runaround." It's the tale of a robot named Speedy (short for SPD-13) and its human masters working on the planet Mercury. The robot is able to speak and think nearly as well as humans thanks to its "positronic" brain. Asimov never explained what a positronic brain was or how it worked, but presumably it had something to do with *positrons*, a kind of subatomic particle.

In "Runaround," Speedy is ordered to travel across the burning hot surface of Mercury to retrieve a rare mineral from a natural pool. Unknown to the robot, the mineral is vital to the survival of its human masters. But the pool, it turns out, gives off a corrosive gas dangerous to the robot. Speedy detects the gas and becomes trapped between the second and third laws. Each time it moves closer to the pool to obey its orders, it must retreat to prevent being damaged by the corrosive gas. Back and forth it goes as time ticks away for the human astronauts.

The astronauts have to venture out into the heat after Speedy to explain

I, ROBOT

Between 1942 and 1985, science-fiction author Isaac Asimov published a series of short stories and at least four novels featuring robots with "positronic brains." These artificial minds gave them near-human intelligence, and in a few cases, telepathic abilities.

By ISAAC ASIMOV

to the robot that if it continues, they will die. Realizing that doing this would violate the first law of robotics, Speedy breaks the loop and gets the mineral, saving the day.

Asimov went on to write many more stories about intelligent robots, and most of them follow the pattern set in "Runaround": a robot ends up in trouble when it falls into a crack between the laws, which—however well reasoned—can't cover every situation. Most of the stories, which were later gathered in a collection called *I, Robot*, were framed as mysteries. The solution of the mystery explained the robots' behavior.

Asimov's three laws are important because they were the first serious consideration of how robots could be kept safe—for themselves and for us. The stories work partly because of the clever puzzles they present and partly because they play on our anxiety over robots. We will almost certainly come to depend on robots, but will we ever learn to trust them entirely?

The First Electronic Brains

Isaac Asimov's ideas were important, but they had no immediate effect on the real world of robotics. That's because there were no positronic brains. No real computer came close to being able to think and make decisions as well as Speedy. In fact, we still can't make such a computer.

All modern computers are made of *switches*, devices that can be in one of two states—open or closed. A series of open and closed switches can be used to represent the numbers used in calculations performed by the computer. The faster the switches can change between the open and closed state, and the more of these switches there are, the faster the computer is.

Human brains use switches called *neurons*, a special kind of cell. They're not very fast, but our brains are made of billions of them. About the time that Asimov was writing his three laws, scientists invented a new kind of electronic switch called a *valve* or *tube*. You may have seen tubes in very old radios. They look a bit like a small light bulb, but they don't give off more than a faint orange glow.

Tubes are much faster than neurons, but they use quite a bit of electricity, get hot, and burn out all the time. The first tube computers were made of tens of thousands of them. They were so big they filled up a whole house! Using this kind of computer to control a robot didn't really seem practical.

Or was it?

17

Robbie the Robot first appeared in the movie *Forbidden Planet* in 1956 and later in dozens of TV shows. This is a staged photograph, and not an actual scene from any movie, but it shows the robot as we would most like it—a servant and a friend to people.

Walter's Tortoise

William Grey Walter was a scientist fascinated by the working of the human brain. When he was very young, he had met Ivan Pavlov, the famous Russian neurophysicist. Later, he helped to develop the *electroencephalograph*—a machine that is still used to measure electrical waves generated in our brains.

Walter wanted to build machines to study certain functions of the brain, and in 1948 he came up with a deceptively simple robot he named *Machina speculatrix*, meaning "the machine that watches." Most people called it the tortoise.

The tortoise had three wheels and a plastic shell. It was controlled by just two motors, two vacuum tubes, and two sensors. The motors were both connected to the front wheel. One drove the wheel around, powering the turtle, while the other one steered the wheel. One of the two sensors could detect light. It was mounted on the steering wheel's

Forbidden Planet (1956)

Robbie, who first appeared in this science-fiction film, is a classic robot: he has the stiff-legged walk, lights that flash in time to his speech, and a formal way of speaking. Through a transparent section of his conical head one can see gears whirring and hear the clatter of relays opening and closing.

Forbidden Planet stars Morbius, a human archeologist who discovers the remains of the Krell, a highly advanced civilization on a solar system 17 light years from Earth. Morbius lives on the Krell home world, alone except for his daughter, Ariel, and Robbie, searching for the answer to a disturbing question: why did the Krell vanish, leaving only their machines?

Robbie plays a key role in the movie. He can manufacture just about any substance in large quantities, cook dinner, and lift several tons—all remarkable accomplishments for a robot without knees.

Like most robots appearing in films, Robbie was really an actor wearing a mechanical suit. The costume was built specifically for the movie *Forbidden Planet* almost 50 years ago by the props department of MGM Studios. It is reported to have cost $125,000, so it was a very expensive prop for its time.

Since its debut in *Forbidden Planet*, the same suit has appeared in dozens of science-fiction films and television shows. Its most recent appearance was in the 2003 movie *Looney Tunes: Back in Action*.

axle and faced in the same direction as the steering wheel. Whenever the sensor detected light, it steered the tortoise towards it. The other sensor was attached to the tortoise's shell. If the shell bumped into anything, it simply stopped the tortoise for a moment. The tortoise would also stop if the light it approached became too bright.

Walter was surprised when the tortoise behaved in animal-like ways that made it seem almost as if it were thinking. If it ran into an object, the tortoise appeared to feel its way around it. Later, Walter mounted a light on the tortoise's shell. If the tortoise was shown a mirror, it would approach it and then do an agitated dance as the tubes rapidly activated and then cut the drive motors, as if it were excited by its own reflection.

The tortoise was the first robot to demonstrate an idea that would surface again years later in the field of artificial intelligence: behaviors that *appear* intelligent can emerge from just a few simple reflexes.

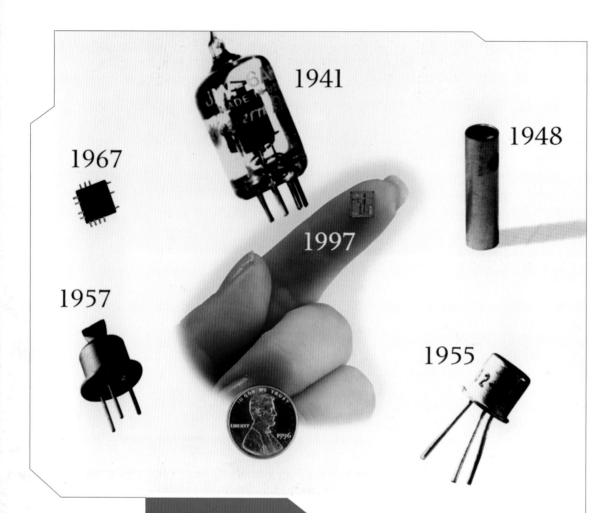

1941

1948

1967

1997

1957

1955

This series of electronic switching devices was used in computers from about 1940 onward. Just above the finger is a vacuum tube—this one used in telephone communications. Moving clockwise is an early point-contact transistor. These were eventually replaced by more modern transistors (1955 and 1957). An early microchip or integrated circuit (1967) contained two transistors in a considerably smaller area. Within three decades, a chip such as the one on the finger could contain as many as 5 million transistors. The question is, will this continual advance in computing power alone be enough to one day produce an intelligent robot?

Solid State Electronics— Small Computers

About the time Walter built his first tortoise, three scientists working for Bell Laboratories—William Shockley, Walter Brattain, and John Bardeen—invented a new kind of switch, the *transistor*. The first transistors were like tiny sandwiches. Each layer had a wire coming out of it. The outer "bread" layers both conducted electricity very well, but the "filling" was made of a material that only conducted electricity if a voltage was sent through its wire.

When this was done, a second current could pass from one bread layer through the filling to the other bread layer. So the filling acted like a gate for electrical current.

The transistor had several advantages over earlier switches: it required very little electricity, it was tiny compared to a tube, and it had no moving parts so it was very reliable. Even better, the transistor could be switched rapidly between the open and closed states—much faster than the tube. It was suddenly possible to build small, complex, and rugged electronic components. Computers began to shrink in size.

Almost overnight, building a robot with a real brain became a possibility.

The Revolution Begins

In 1956, two self-taught inventors, Joe Engelberger and George DeVol, met at a party. The conversation soon turned to a common interest: the science-fiction writings of Isaac Asimov, and in particular his robot stories.

The inventors embarked on a project to build a real machine that could do the work of a human factory worker. They began by visiting about 20 factories and looking at the various jobs. They soon realized that most workers were simply picking up parts from one place and moving them to another. Engelberger and DeVol thought they could build a machine able to do this by using the new solid state electronics, and became business partners.

They called their new company Unimation—a combination of the words *universal* and *automation*. The machine they eventually designed was a mechanical arm that rotated

21

As the robot revolution was getting underway here on Earth, the United States and the Soviet Union began sending machines into space—first into orbit and later to the moon.

The earliest lunar probes were little more than flying cameras. They either snapped pictures as they hurtled past the moon or smashed into its surface, collecting images until the moment of impact. In 1966 a Soviet probe, *Luna 9*, made the first soft landing on the lunar surface. It took thousands of photographs using a panoramic camera.

The first truly robotic probe was probably the United States' *Surveyor 7*, which had a mechanical arm ending in a scoop. Operating on commands from scientists in Houston, it scooped up a shovelful of lunar dirt and discovered that it was about the consistency of wet beach sand. Until that time, some scientists believed the lunar surface might be covered with a dust so fine and deep that a spaceship landing there would sink without a trace!

After the Apollo program had landed astronauts on the moon in 1969, the Soviets landed the mobile space probe *Lunokhod 1* on the lunar surface. It looked a bit like an eight-wheeled baby buggy. From November 1970 to October 1971, it collected over 500 soil samples and took some 20,000 photographs.

on a pedestal. It also had a shoulder and an elbow that could pivot up and down. At the end of the arm was a "hand" (really just a clamp that could open and close), which could be positioned anywhere within the arm's reach. They called their robotic arm Unimate.

Unimate weighed as much as a minivan and could lift an object weighing up to 34 kilograms (75 pounds). Engelberger and DeVol "taught" Unimate the necessary motions by manually moving the mechanical arm to each new position required. Every time they moved the arm, Unimate recorded the new position on a magnetic drum inside its pedestal. The robot could then play back the entire sequence of movements as often as needed.

Unimate went to work in 1961 at a General Motors die-casting factory in New Jersey. The robotic arm took pieces of hot metal from dies (molds) and stacked them. Later, it was adapted to welding car parts together. Unimate was the first industrial robot to be controlled by an electronic computer.

Although it looked nothing like a person, Unimate was the laborer that Rossum Junior had dreamed of 40 years earlier. It never tired or complained about its work. Nor did it ever ask for a raise. But most importantly, when a factory stopped making one product and switched to another, it did not have to be replaced by a different machine; it could simply be reprogrammed to grasp a different part and move it in a different pattern. Alternatively, its hand could be traded for a welder or a spray gun. This resulted in huge cost savings for its operators. It held particular promise for car makers, who have a habit of making alterations to the models they produce every year.

After their initial success at General Motors, however, Engelberger and DeVol found industrial robots to be a hard sell in North America. Most manufacturers just didn't see the point in replacing workers with very expensive machines.

Then, in 1968, Engelberger was invited to Japan, where his ideas were received with much greater enthusiasm. That same year Unimation licensed the technology behind their robotic arms to Kawasaki Heavy Industries. Over the next 20 years, many Japanese companies began to develop their own factory robots, and by the middle of the 1980s Japan had over 100,000 of them. In contrast, the United States had only about one-quarter this number.

It's a lead that Japan has never lost. To this day, it has more robots than all of the other nations of the world combined. Its huge robotic labor force is one of the reasons Japanese products are among the best built in the world.

Seeing the success of the robot arm, others turned their attention to building robot legs. In 1967, Ralph Mosher from General Electric developed a four-legged "walking truck" with funding from the United States Department of Defense. The walking truck looked a bit like a headless mechanical camel, with the operator seated inside a cockpit where the hump would be. It's said to have been the inspiration for the Imperial walkers that appeared in the Star Wars movie *The Empire Strikes Back*. Like Unimate, the walking truck's joints were powered by electric motors.

Although a human operator pushed pedals to steer the truck and urge it forward, simple electronics coordinated the motions of the individual legs. Its top speed was—well, about walking speed for a person. But walking proved to be a much more difficult task than using an arm. Not only did it mean controlling four times as many limbs, but while doing that, the robot had to keep its balance. When an animal walks, its brain must keep track of the positions of its legs and feet and the many forces acting upon them. And the animal repeats this process many times a second as it moves. This means processing a lot of information.

For a robot—especially one weighing more than most cars and using primitive computers—walking was a tough act to follow. Mosher's design didn't offer any practical advantages over wheeled vehicles, but as one of the first walking machines it was, quite literally, an important step forward in robotics.

Shakey

In 1968, Nils Nillson was working at the Stanford Research Institute, where he designed and built Shakey. Shakey was about the size of a water cooler.

It moved around on wheels and navigated through a combination of vision (using a camera mounted on top of it) and feel (using a set of whiskers that stuck out of its front).

There was nothing remarkable about Shakey's body. It had no limbs of any kind; all Shakey did was roll around the floor of its lab. When-ever it stopped or started, it wobbled back and forth on its wheels, hence its name. Its claim to fame was its brain and eyes. Shakey was able to view its surroundings through a videocamera and analyze the picture using a large computer in the next room. Information was sent between the computer and the robot via radio waves.

Shakey was the first robot to have a low-level artificial intelligence, thanks to computer programming. It could maneuver through doorways, detect obstacles with its videocamera, avoid them, and even push boxes from one location to another.

This made Shakey the first robot to do more than just follow a program; it could make decisions and modify its own programming based on information it gathered from the world around it. With the creation of early computer-controlled machines like Shakey, scientists began to realize the potential of computers, but also the magnitude of the task that lay before them in creating a true robot.

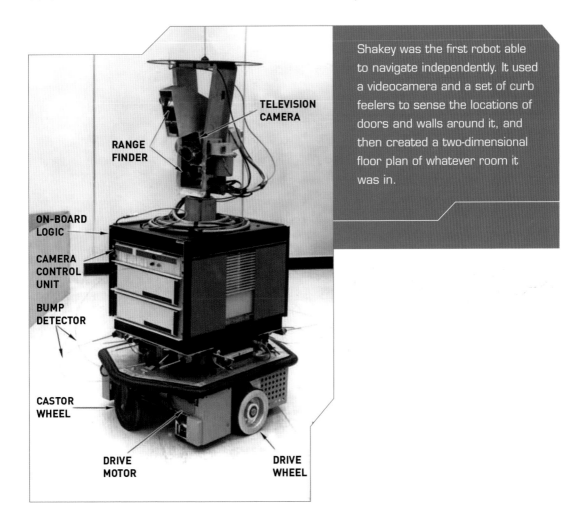

RANGE FINDER

TELEVISION CAMERA

ON-BOARD LOGIC

CAMERA CONTROL UNIT

BUMP DETECTOR

CASTOR WHEEL

DRIVE MOTOR

DRIVE WHEEL

Shakey was the first robot able to navigate independently. It used a videocamera and a set of curb feelers to sense the locations of doors and walls around it, and then created a two-dimensional floor plan of whatever room it was in.

Wabot-1

By 1970, scientists had invented robot legs, robotic arms, and electronic cameras that could serve as crude artificial eyes. It was probably inevitable that someone would try to put them all together in a working, humanoid robot. The first serious attempt was made by scientists and students at Waseda University in Japan. In 1970, they began work on Wabot-1. This robot had basic hearing and vision, and rudimentary verbal skills. It could walk—although taking one step was a 45-second process—and had a crude sense of touch in its hands.

Wabot-1's makers likened its mental abilities to those of a one-and-a-half-year-old child, but that was probably an exaggeration. Although it was not particularly good at any one thing, Wabot-1 was the most ambitious robot built to that time, and it became a symbol of Japan's determination to become the world leader in robotics.

What's Next?

So where does that leave us, nearly three centuries after de Vaucanson's flute player and more than three decades after Wabot-1?

Real robots have become essential to industry, warfare, and the exploration of space and our oceans. They have accomplished many things but they are still far from the robots of our imagination. Certainly the dream of the mechanical servant seems as remote as ever. There isn't a robot yet that can do so much as fetch you a glass of water.

Robots today are a bit like Frankenstein's monster, still lying on a table in the laboratory. All of the pieces have been sewn together. Beneath the sheet, we can make out the contours of a body a little like our own, but it awaits some essential spark to animate it.

For Dr. Frankenstein, it was a bolt of lightning that gave his creature life. For roboticists, that spark will almost certainly be a breakthrough in the field of artificial intelligence. That breakthrough may take the form of a revolutionary computer or a new programming language. Like lightning, we cannot know when it will strike. But when it does, the creature will rise from the slab.

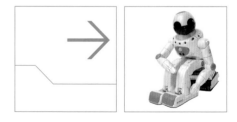

chapter 2

Where Are All the Robots?

When people living 40 years ago tried to imagine what our lives would be like today, they often envisioned a world filled with robots. The animated television series *The Jetsons* is a good example. Most episodes of *The Jetsons* told of everyday events in the life of George Jetson, an office worker, and his family, who lived in the then-distant future.

The Jetsons' house was supported on very long legs and had a glass bubble for a roof. Almost all buildings in this future floated high in the air, and people traveled between them in flying cars. Each morning, George's bed would wake him up, toss him onto the floor, make itself, and then fold into the wall so that George couldn't go back to sleep. Robotic arms would pull off his pajamas and dress him. In the bathroom, another set of arms would squeeze toothpaste onto a brush and move it back and forth across his teeth; all George had to do was stand in front of the mirror and open his mouth.

In the kitchen, Jane Jetson was already busy preparing breakfast for her family by adding a drop of water to a pill that sprouted into a complete meal.

The family was also served by a robot maid named Rosie. Rosie looked a little like a person. She had a head, arms, and hands like a

27

lobster's pincers. Instead of legs, she rolled around the house on wheels, doing her chores—although with all the helpful devices around, it's hard to imagine what would be left for a maid to do.

The Jetsons was not a serious look at the future, but it reflected the beliefs held at the time it was made—the early 1960s. People thought that by now robots would be making our lives easier by giving us more time to play and relax. Although George had an office job at Spacely Sprockets, he spent most of his three-hour workday snoozing in a chair with his feet up on the desk.

Of course, *The Jetsons* was a poor prediction of the future. Forty years after it was first broadcast, no one flies his car to work and most of us are still brushing our own teeth. Why *don't* we all have robots in our homes? Wouldn't people be happy to have mechanical servants washing the dishes, vacuuming the floors, and making their beds?

Good Help Is Hard to Make

It turns out that building robots able to work in our homes is much more difficult than scientists first thought. To give you an idea of the problems involved, let's imagine a household robot designed to do one simple thing: make you a bowl of cereal for breakfast.

You begin by stumbling from your bedroom to the kitchen and muttering the word "Cheerios" to your CerealMaster 3000 robotic breakfast machine. The first thing your robotic servant must do is hear and understand your command. It must recognize the word "Cheerios" and be able to tell that word from "Shredded Wheat" or "Corn Flakes" or about 80 different prepared cereals that you can buy in a super-market. Let's assume that this part of the task goes well. We already have telephones that will dial someone's number if you speak the name clearly, so it isn't too hard to believe.

Knowing that it must now find the Cheerios, the CerealMaster starts looking for the box. But suppose this is the CerealMaster's first day on the job. Where does it start looking? You and I know that most people keep their cereal in a kitchen cupboard, but that information would have to be programmed into the robot.

Now that we're on the subject of cupboards, how do you open one? If the cupboard has a handle, you just pull on it, right? But how hard? And how exactly do you know when to *stop* opening a cupboard (preferably before it comes off the hinges)? And how will the CerealMaster tell a

The Daleks are evil robots that appeared in several episodes of the long-running British science-fiction television series *Dr. Who*. As each Dalek actually contains an alien from the planet Skaro, they are technically cybernetic organisms, and not robots. This one is taking time out from its fiendish plans for world domination to collect charitable donations on a London street.

handle from a hinge, so that it knows which way the door opens? It could store a picture of a handle in its brain, but not all handles look alike. In fact, there are tens of thousands of different kinds. Come to think of it, a handle doesn't always look the same. In the morning, the light from the kitchen window casts a shadow of the handle across the cupboard door. At night, the ceiling light hardly casts any shadow at all. How can a robot tell where the handle ends and the shadow begins?

As you can see, a simple task like serving a bowl of cereal is not so simple—and we haven't even got to the problem of opening a milk carton! The task has many, many steps. A person can perform most of those steps without even thinking— at least consciously. That's because people spend the first few years of their lives learning about kitchens, handles, shadows, and everything else in the world.

29

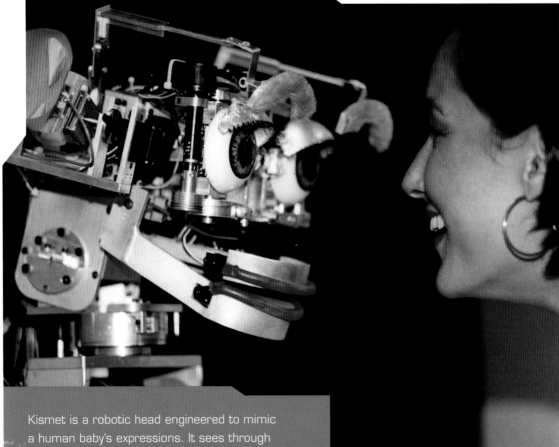

Kismet is a robotic head engineered to mimic a human baby's expressions. It sees through videocameras and can react to objects and people with smiles, frowns, and movements of its ears and eyebrows. Here it's shown with Cynthia Breazeal, its inventor. By observing how people and Kismet interact, Breazeal hopes to discover how very young children learn about the world.

You probably opened your first cupboard when you were a baby, and you did it just by putting your hands on it and pushing and pulling until something moved. That's how babies learn about the world. It's why they are always grasping things and trying to cram them in their mouths or bash them against the floor. You may have tried to pick up a shadow at some point too, but eventually you learned that it's a waste of time.

A practical household robot would have to be programmed with knowledge of the world inside the house before it could function at all like a person. Either that or it would have to be able to learn in much the way a baby does—by trying things.

And who wants a robot smashing, shaking, and rattling things around the house to find out how they work?

The problem with trying to program everything into a robot's brain is that we don't know what "everything" is—that is, no one has ever written down everything that people know. Oh sure, we've written down the things that we think are important—like when the first person landed on the moon, or who invented TV, or the names of all the countries in the world. But no one has ever sat down and written out all the truly *basic* stuff that each of us knows—like the fact that electrician's tape makes a poor dessert topping, or no, I haven't seen your blue jacket anywhere, or a shadow is usually darker than the object casting it. There are just too many facts in the world to list!

Because we can't say all that we know, we can't even begin to tell a robot everything it needs to know to operate in the world.

So by now you may be thinking, "But the cereal box was probably made by a robot, or some kind of machine anyway. If machines can *make* a cereal box, then finding a cereal box and opening it should be easy for them."

It's true that automatic machines would have printed the label on the cardboard, cut the cardboard into a precise shape, smeared glue on parts of it, and then folded it into a box.

But these machines were not working inside a kitchen; they were in a factory—a place designed especially for making and filling cereal boxes.

Probably no single machine made the box. Instead, there was a series of machines arranged in a particular order. Such a series of machines (or people) is called an assembly line. Typically, each machine in an assembly line performs only one simple action—like gluing or folding. Upon completing its action, the machine passes the partially made box on to the next machine. When the last machine in the line has finished doing whatever it does, the box is finished.

And so these automatic machines do not have to sense the world around them or know anything about it. They don't have to go looking for the cardboard or the inks needed to make the box. They don't have to make decisions. They just perform their one function, over and over again—something that machines do very well.

That is why robots make great factory workers. But to build a true general-purpose robot like Rosie the maid would be far more difficult. Making her will require even further advances in computer science—and until then, you will be making your own breakfast.

Does that mean we will never make a robot as capable as a human being? We still don't know.

Did we say that there are just too many facts in the world to list? That hasn't stopped some people from trying. For the last 20 years, Doug Lenat has been working on the Cyc Project, a $60 million attempt to create an artificial brain with something no computer has: common sense. Since 1984, Lenat and a team of theologians, mathematicians, philosophers, and linguists have been entering general knowledge about life, the universe, and everything into a computer database— one statement at a time.

Here is an example of the kinds of assertions being entered into Cyc's database:

Fifi is a common name for a poodle.

All poodles are dogs.

A dog has four legs unless it has had an accident or surgery.

Told that "Fifi has three legs," Cyc could then generate a fourth assertion, "Fifi has probably had an accident or surgery."

It uses a special computer program called an inference engine to connect assertions and draw conclusions. Literally millions of common-sense assertions have been typed into the Cyc database.

How does the team choose which assertions to enter? Lenat began by reading passages from books at random and then trying to list every assumption the author would have had to make in writing the passage.

Cyc is encouraged to ask questions if it needs clarification of any of the data entered into it. Already it has asked some good ones,

including "Am I human?" That happened just two years into the project. Later that same year it asked if any other computers were working on the project.

Will Cyc result in an intelligent computer? Not all by itself. But Lenat and the other 60 members of the Cyc team are optimistic that their database will have widespread applications.

One of Lenat's assertions is that the average person knows about 100 million things about the world. In 2002, he predicted that Cyc would reach that level of knowledge in approximately 2007. Currently, Cyc contains just over 3.4 million assertions, so the project is behind schedule. But Cyc is being given access to the Internet. People will be able to ask Cyc questions, then correct any wrong answers it gives. Lenat believes this will greatly accelerate Cyc's acquisition of knowledge.

Top Down or Bottom Up?

Currently, the science of artificial intelligence takes two basic approaches. The first is called the "top-down" approach. The followers of this method argue that intelligence is the result of our brains' ability to manipulate symbols. Computers also operate by manipulating symbols. In theory, all we have to do is figure out the symbol-manipulation program running in our brains and then write a similar program for an electronic computer. Unfortunately, if there is such a program running in our brains, we're still far from understanding it. We can only guess at how human beings form thoughts, reason, and make decisions.

Other researchers believe that the top-down approach is hopeless, and that the human mind can never understand itself. They believe our best hope of creating an artificial intelligence is to program a robot with a few simple rules to control its behavior in the real world (much like Walter's tortoise) but give it the ability to modify those rules based on its successes and failures. In this way, it would evolve and learn, much as intelligence evolved over time in biological organisms. This is called the "bottom-up" approach.

To date, neither approach has been very successful. The top-down approach has resulted in some computer programs that do things like diagnose diseases or play chess. These so-called "expert systems" have been very successful within their narrow, academic scopes, so we now have machines able to play chess or identify illnesses better than any single human being. But no one has been able to write a program that enables a robot to function in the real world with even the skill of an ant.

Researchers using the bottom-up approach have tried to duplicate the behavior of some primitive organisms. One project aimed to emulate the behavior of a species of worm that has only 300 neurons in its brain (by comparison, our own brains have billions of neurons). This too has failed.

None of this means that researchers are giving up. But instead of trying to reproduce the full range of human abilities, most are just trying to build machines that do one or two things really well.

In 1986, the Honda Corporation— the company that makes the cars and motorcycles—began a secret project. Its goal was to develop a general-purpose robot for use in the home. It has taken them almost 20 years and, some estimate, over 100 million dollars, but they've made real progress. The Honda scientists decided to work first on the robot's ability to walk, as an essential step in building a robot able to move freely about the home and interact naturally with human beings.

The original P1 prototype, which Honda unveiled in 1993, had arms and legs like a person, but in place of a head and neck was a large featureless block. P1 was the size of an adult human being, weighed twice as much, and was powered by electricity delivered through cables hung from the ceiling. Although it could walk quite well, it had to stop momentarily before changing direction or speed and was controlled by an operator with a remote control.

ASIMO, unveiled in the year 2000, is the eighth prototype in the series and it looks a bit like an astronaut wearing a space helmet and the typical, bulky backpack. However, it's only about the size of a seven-year-old child and carries its own power supply. With each new prototype, the engineers have reduced the robot's size so that it will be less intimidating to people but still tall enough to operate a faucet or a light switch. ASIMO can't do either of those things yet, but its designers are clearly thinking ahead. The name ASIMO stands for Advanced Step in Innovative Mobility but, as you may have noticed, it almost spells Asimov—

Working from the Top Down

Marvin Minsky of the Massachusetts Institute of Technology was one of the first scientists to realize the problem of robots knowing nothing about the real world. In 1968, he built a robot consisting of a mechanical arm, a television camera, and a computer to control them. He programmed the computer to recognize a stack of children's blocks through the camera's lens and memorize their positions. Then he knocked over the stack and ordered the robot to rebuild it exactly as it had been before.

The robot quickly found the block that had been at the top of the stack, picked it up, placed it in midair exactly where it had been, and then let go. Of course, the block fell to the floor. The robot just kept picking up the same block and dropping it in midair. Minsky's robot did not know what every child knows: any object that isn't supported from below falls to the ground.

the name of the writer who invented the three laws of robotics.

When ASIMO is standing still, it does so with its knees slightly flexed, like a skier. This helps it to keep its balance. It is ASIMO's ability to balance that makes it the most advanced of all walking robots. It has sensors in its torso that let its computer brain know if it is standing upright or tilting. If someone gently pushes on its face, these sensors tell the robot that it is about to topple, and it takes a step back to keep itself from falling over.

And that's really how walking works. When we walk, we bring a leg forward and, because we're soon off balance, we start to fall over. We plant the leading foot on the ground to keep from falling, push off with the trailing leg, pivot on the forward leg as we bring the trailing leg forward, and then start to topple over again. It's a process of starting to fall over and then recovering, repeated over and over. This is known as dynamic walking.

ASIMO walks dynamically. Sensors on different parts of the soles of ASIMO's feet measure pressure. A computer brain monitors the input from these sensors as well as the tilt sensors in the chest and then causes ASIMO to adjust its stride if it is ordered to turn, stop, or walk faster.

The joints where the robot's legs meet its hips move not only

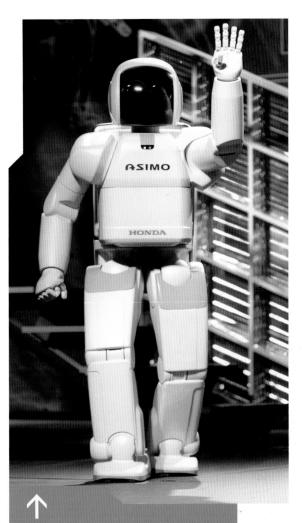

↑

Asimo is the Honda Corporation's latest in a series of prototype robots. After working on the project for over 20 years, Honda has created a child-sized robot that walks amazingly well. In doing so, its inventors have cleared a major hurdle to developing a multi-purpose robot that might one day work in our homes.

Minority Report is set in a city approximately 50 years from now. In this world, automobiles are controlled entirely by computer. Rather than parking in garages, they climb giant apartment buildings, each car becoming an enclosed balcony for its driver's apartment. Advertisements address potential customers by name, and people's whereabouts are constantly monitored by retinal scanners.

The film's main character, John Anderton, is a policeman falsely accused of murder and on the run from his fellow officers. At one point the police send a squad of tiny spiderlike robots to search an old apartment building for him. The "spiderbots" appear to be somewhat intelligent, and have good hearing and vision.

The idea of modeling robots on animal bodies is not a new one. Scientists have already made robots in the forms of snakes, tuna, lobsters, and insects. The spider body is an excellent choice for a search robot. Real spiders are able to find their way into almost any building by climbing up drainpipes, along walls, and over ceilings. A small robot also has the advantage of being able to search a building without alerting its quarry.

A spiderbot does eventually find Anderton. In its memory, the robot carries a record of the pattern of the blood vessels in Anderton's retina, and it attempts to identify him by shining a light into his eye and comparing his eye with the record. But Anderton has

had his eyes surgically replaced so that he won't be identified by such means. The spiderbot eventually scans his eyes but fails to identify him.

The spiderbots, with their bulbous bodies, stealthy movements, and wire-thin legs, are well beyond today's technology—so much so that even to make working models or puppets of them wasn't possible. Instead, they exist only as images on film—the result of computer animation.

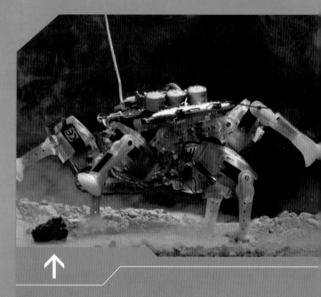

↑

A small six-legged robot crawls across a simulated alien landscape. NASA has experimented with many robot designs employing legs, but all of their actual rover missions have used wheeled vehicles. While legs are more versatile, wheels are faster, easier to control, and more reliable.

backwards and forwards, but from side to side, just like a human being's. This enables it to move quite naturally. In fact, most people's first impression upon seeing the robot is that it's a child wearing a suit. It's astonishing, and a little bit eerie. ASIMO even goes up and down stairs—although the steps must be of a precise size and it must be started in just the right spot at either the top or bottom of the staircase, or it will stumble.

While internal computers control ASIMO's ability to walk and balance, its direction of travel is still determined by operators using remote controls. The Honda engineers next plan to concentrate on improving their robot's ability to see. Currently, ASIMO can turn its head towards a human voice and shake hands. It has the ability to recognize up to 12 human faces.

The latest ASIMO model has taken up running. The main difference between walking and running is that, at times during running, both feet leave the ground. Watching ASIMO run reminds you of your 80-year-old grandfather out for a jog—he takes quick little steps, knees bent, and hardly moves any faster than he does walking. But when you're 80 years old and still jogging, people aren't likely to criticize your style; rather, they marvel that you can jog at all. The same could be said for a robot.

Qrio (pronounced "curio") is the Sony's Corporation's counterpart to Asimo. Although capable of a wider variety of movements, Qrio is less than half the size of Asimo, and designed strictly for entertainment.

Rodney Brooks is a leader in the field of artificial intelligence, known for both his brilliance and his crankiness. Many of his fellow scientists disagree with his theories, which seem to go against the common wisdom. No one can deny, however, that his ideas have produced results. Some of his programs were incorporated in the *Sojourner* rover, which traveled to Mars in 1997.

Brooks is of the bottom-up school of AI. Like many researchers taking this approach, he thinks that attempts to build a computer brain endowed with all of the higher functions we think of as human— self-awareness, planning and creating goals, getting brain freeze from gulping milkshakes—will never work.

But Brooks takes the bottom-up school a step further: he actually believes that there is *no such thing* as the "higher intelligence" that supposedly accounts for the most complex human and animal behaviors. Rather, our behaviors are just the result of combinations of automatic responses to the world. In short, he feels that intelligence is overrated.

You can see why Brooks might not be too popular with some of his fellow scientists. How would you feel about someone who told you that something you've spent your life searching for doesn't even exist?

Brooks's view of intelligence is something like the way we think about ants or bees. They do some amazing things—such as building complicated nests and raising their young and protecting their hives from intruders—but nobody believes that any individual ant or bee is planning ahead or thinking about how to do all of this. There is no single brain in control of the hive or anthill. Instead, each bee or ant reacts to things around it, and somehow it all just works.

To test his theory, Brooks and a series of graduate students at the Massachusetts Institute of Tech- nology have been working on a robot called Cog for the last 10 years. The idea is to give Cog the ability to react to people at approximately the level of a six-month-old human baby. Although Cog looks nothing like a baby, it does bear some resemblance to the human form. It has a head, torso, and arms. No legs, though.

Brooks has started by programming Cog to do some of the things a baby does. When a person enters the room, Cog can follow her with its "eyes" (a pair of videocameras) and reach towards her. It can also imitate people's hand movements.

Cog is another robotic torso that, like Kismet, was developed at the Massachusetts Institute of Technology as an aid to creating an artificial intelligence. The man whose head it is gripping is Rodney Brooks, its inventor.

Brooks is also studying how people react to Cog. Seeing the robot's responses, most people find it very difficult to shake the idea that Cog is aware of its surroundings. Clearly, Cog is not conscious in the way a human being is, but Brooks believes that this only proves his point: awareness is something we attribute to people and other animals. It's a useful description, but that doesn't prove it exists.

But is any of this getting us closer to an intelligent robot? It's hard to tell. Cog doesn't yet show anything like intelligence, and Brooks seems evasive when asked about concrete results. He keeps talking about how people who meet Cog in person react to its movements as if it were an intelligent being—not a surprising response from a man who believes there's no such thing as an intelligent being. When asked how long it will be before his project pays off, Brooks says,

39

"Maybe 50 years, maybe 10 years."
Then he reconsiders: "Ten years
is too optimistic."

Marvin Minsky (see sidebar,
page 34) would probably agree.
In a speech he made in 2003 he
declared that "AI has been brain-
dead since the 1970s . . . The worst
fad has been these stupid little
robots. Graduate students are
wasting three years of their lives
soldering and repairing robots,
instead of making them smart. It's
really shocking."

That's a matter of opinion.
Intelligence evolved in animals
over millions of years through their
interaction with each other and
the world around them. Whether
Brooks can cause a machine to "get
smart" within 50 years is debatable,
but it's one approach.

Robonaut

Robonaut is NASA's effort to build a
robot with the dexterity of a human
astronaut. It must be able to do most
of the things that a human being
wearing a pressure suit can do,
using the same tools that the astronauts would use on a spacewalk.

Like Cog, Robonaut is currently
just a head and torso. Unlike
Cog, Robonaut is a tele-operated
robot—a person directly controls all
of its actions from a distance. The
operator wears a visor over his face.
Small video screens facing the
operator's eyes allow him to see
what Robonaut sees through its two
videocameras. The operator also
wears sleeves and gloves covered
with sensors in strategic locations.
These sensors can "feel" the movement of the operator's hands and
arms, and transmit the signals to
Robonaut, which exactly duplicates
the movements of the operator.

But it's Robonaut's hands that
are truly special. Like human hands,
each has four fingers and a thumb.
All of the fingers have at least one
degree of freedom—that is, each
of the "knuckles" can bend back
and forth. The index and middle
fingers both have an additional
degree of freedom, meaning they
can also bend from side to side
where they join the palm, just like
human fingers.

The fingers are operated by cables
running from 14 motors housed in
the forearm. Sensors in the fingertips measure the pressure exerted by
the hand on whatever it is grasping
and feed the information back to the
operator's gloves. The operator
then experiences the sensation
of gripping whatever it is that
Robonaut is gripping.

Of course, Robonaut is more than
just its hands. The space inside the

Here's Robonaut mounted on a modified Segway. A Segway is a wheeled platform that looks a little like an old push lawn mower. You step on the part of the mower where the blades would be, and roll from place to place. Segway is able to balance, so it can support Robonaut (which has no legs) without tipping over. Such an arrangement would be useless in the weightlessness of space, but it's a practical way for Robonaut to get around on Earth.

→

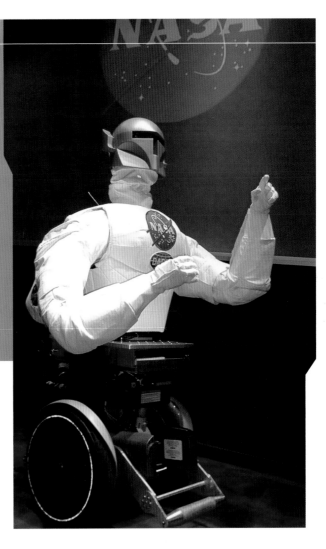

head is taken up mostly by two cameras that give the robot stereovision. Most animals with eyes close together on the front of the face—like people, monkeys, and owls—have stereovision. When each eye has a slightly different view of the same object, the brain can judge how far away the object is and see it in three dimensions. Judging distances accurately is crucial when working with tools or parts in space.

Robonaut's head is mounted on a flexible neck that can tilt forward or from side to side, giving the cameras (and their tele-operator) a good view of the surroundings. They can also zoom in for close-up views.

Robonaut's computer brain is actually located inside the torso, where it is better protected from the

harsh conditions of outer space and from collisions with other objects. The rechargeable batteries are also housed in the chest. One way that Robonaut might operate is with its torso attached to the Space Shuttle's robotic arm—like a telephone-line repairman in a bucket hoist.

There are certain advantages to building a robot for use in space. For one, despite the term "spacewalk," there's no actual walking involved, as

41

astronauts float from place to place. So you don't have to worry about your robot keeping its balance. Also, trying to match the dexterity of an astronaut wearing spacesuit gloves is a lot easier than trying to match the dexterity of a naked human hand.

And a robot's spacewalk time isn't limited by an oxygen supply or the need for bathroom breaks. Just getting into a spacesuit and preparing for a spacewalk takes a human astronaut almost three hours!

But making a robot that can work in space also presents special difficulties. Motors and joints must be able to operate in a vacuum as well as in extremes of temperature. This calls for special lubricants and materials that don't expand and contract too much with heat and cold. Most of Robonaut's work, such as repairing satellites, will probably be done in Earth's orbit. But if it ever ventures beyond the Earth's magnetic field, circuit boards and microprocessors will have to be protected from cosmic radiation.

Three Different Goals

ASIMO, Cog, and Robonaut are all on the leading edge of robotics. Robonaut will almost certainly work in space. ASIMO, with the resources of a large and wealthy corporation behind it, has a good chance of reaching the market and one day functioning as a robot assistant in the home. Already, Honda will rent it to anyone willing to pay their rate of $20,000 US a day.

Whether Cog will lead to a robot that can act independently is anyone's guess, but many scientists are skeptical. Yet Cog is really the most ambitious of the three projects. It is an attempt not only to advance the science of artificial intelligence, but to understand the most mysterious and complex thing science has encountered—the human mind.

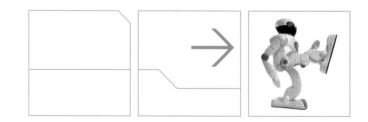

chapter 3
Robot Explorers

Robots have their limitations, but there is one way in which they are superior to human beings: they're a lot tougher than we are. They can withstand extremes of temperature, radiation, and pressure that would kill a person. As long as they're switched off, they don't require fuel. They can wait folded up in a box for months or years until the moment they're needed. Robots can go where people can't, and they do it without fear or complaint. For all these reasons, robots, with a little human guidance, are exploring the limits of our universe.

Robots have been highly successful in exploring both inner and outer space. In 1995, a Japanese remotely operated vehicle reached the deepest point in all the world's oceans—10,911 meters (36,000 feet) below sea level. The manned space program began in the late 1950s and within 10 short years the Apollo program triumphed by landing more than a dozen astronauts on the surface of the moon. But since then, space exploration has been handed over almost entirely to unmanned probes.

One of them, *Voyager I*, was launched nearly 30 years ago to gather information about Jupiter and Saturn, but it is still working today, sending data on solar radiation back to NASA scientists.

That's a pretty impressive record, especially when you consider that *Voyager* has about 65,000 parts, which present a lot of possibilities for failure. As the probe passed Jupiter, it withstood radiation a thousand times the level that would kill an unprotected human being. *Voyager* has traveled 13.6 billion kilometers (8.5 billion miles) and is now more than three times as far from the Earth as the planet Pluto.

Closer to home, space probes have also sent back data about Venus, and one will soon be studying Mercury. But the planet most thoroughly explored by robotic probes is our closest planetary neighbor, Mars.

The Americans and Russians have been sending robotic probes to Mars for 40 years now. Fully half of them have either crashed or been lost in space. The most recent failure was Britain's first robotic probe to Mars, *Beagle 2*. In late 2003 it entered the atmosphere of Mars, but it hasn't been heard from since. Scientists believe it probably crashed on the Martian surface.

Obviously, sending a robot to Mars isn't easy, but there have been great successes. The *Mariner* probes of the 1960s photographed the Martian surface and even a giant dust storm that enveloped the entire planet as the probe flew by. In 1976, the *Viking* probe made a soft landing on Mars, collected a scoopful of soil using a mechanical arm, put it into a box, added water and nutrients, then incubated the dirt in the hope of finding signs of microscopic life. Scientists are still arguing over the results of that experiment. Today, most agree that *Viking* failed to prove there is life on Mars.

 ## *Spirit* and *Opportunity* on Mars

The rovers *Spirit* and *Opportunity* are the latest robots to visit the red planet. These twin tractors were sent on separate ships to different parts of Mars, trips that took almost seven months. In the first few days of 2004, the vessel carrying *Spirit* entered the Martian atmosphere at almost 5½ kilometers (3½ miles) per second—faster than a rifle bullet. It slowed itself down through friction with the thin Martian atmosphere, a technique known as *aerobraking*. About three minutes later, a mortar fired a parachute up and away from the probe to slow its descent to about 75 meters (250 feet) per second. That's still quite fast— about twice highway speed. Because the Martian atmosphere is so thin, a parachute can't slow an object down as well as it could on Earth, so the parachute was cut free and a pair of rocket motors fired, bringing the

The *Voyager 1* space probe, launched in 1977, is now the farthest manmade object from planet Earth. After three decades and 13.6 billion kilometers (8.5 billion miles) of space travel, this robot continues to return useful data to scientists on its journey far beyond the edge of our solar system.

Robot Explorers

ship to a halt about 15 meters (50 feet) above the planet's surface. Finally, an airbag surrounding the probe inflated and the probe was cut loose, dropping it to the ground. It came bouncing to a halt on target, in Gusev Crater.

Gusev Crater is about 160 kilometers (100 miles) in diameter, and scientists believe it may have once been the site of a Martian lake. A big part of *Spirit*'s mission was to search for signs of ancient water, and this was thought to be a good starting point.

After its rough ride, *Spirit* sent home a series of signals and a few snapshots of the Martian surface, just to let everyone on Earth know it had landed safely. While the scientists at NASA shook hands and slapped each other on the back, *Spirit* began deflating its airbags, opening the "petals"—a series of ramps leading from the landing vehicle—and unfolding the rover's solar panels. It also sent up its periscope-like camera mast to get a better look at its surroundings.

And then *Spirit* did what any good

45

explorer would: it took a nap to conserve battery power.

All these actions were controlled by computers aboard the space probe. This is far more reliable than trying to send commands from Earth. Even if you could align an antenna so that *Spirit* would always be in contact with Houston, signals would take 10 minutes to reach it—Mars is a long way away! Once the probe began exploring, additional instructions would be sent from Earth.

It took a full week for *Spirit* to extend its wheels and roll off the landing platform. This is because *Spirit* is the most complicated robot ever made. A whole variety of systems had to be tested and each of its nine cameras activated. Most of these cameras are used to avoid running into obstacles. The other four sit atop the rover's mast, giving it a view similar to that of a person standing up.

Another reason it took so long to move off the landing platform is that part of the lander's protective airbag refused to deflate completely, blocking the rover's path. The scientists then had to figure out another route off the lander to make sure the rover wouldn't catch on the fabric.

Finally the time came for *Spirit* to leave its nest. Before it could begin rolling, small explosive devices were detonated to cut the 12 cables anchoring it to the landing platform.

To conserve power and avoid collisions, the rover's top speed is only about five centimeters (two inches) per second. If *Spirit* should tip over or snag on something, there is no one to help it out. Such a disaster would put an end to its mission. Slowly, *Spirit* backed down one of the ramps leading from the platform.

One of *Spirit*'s first tasks after moving away from the lander was to deploy its manipulator arm. This is about the size of a human arm and also has shoulder, elbow, and wrist joints, for a total of five degrees of freedom. Instead of a hand, at the end of the arm is a turret on which are mounted four different instruments: a microscope, two spectrometers, and the rock abrasion tool, or RAT. The RAT is used to grind away rock to create a fresh, flat surface for examination. The spectrometers identify the chemical makeup of different substances. The microscope is for looking at soil and rocks up close.

All of *Spirit*'s tools are geared towards examining Mars's geology, because, other than the weather, that's about all there is to look at: dirt and rocks. There are certainly no plants or animals to study—at least not on the planet's surface. It's too dry and too cold to support the kind of life we have on Earth.

Spirit was in the middle of examining its first rock with one

of the spectrometers when it developed a problem: its main computer began rebooting over and over. Scientists were worried that it would soon drain its batteries and be unable to do anything. Eventually they traced the problem to the computer's flash memory, and programmers were able to send it a command to stop it from rebooting. It took them weeks to reload new software and get the rover working normally again.

In the meantime, the second Mars rover, *Opportunity*, landed on the

The European Space Agency's *Beagle 2* probe was supposed to land on Mars on Christmas Day, 2003. Unfortunately, all contact with the lander was lost shortly after it separated from the orbiter that had delivered it to Mars. It probably crashed, but it may have landed safely and be unable to communicate for some reason. Mission scientists have used cameras orbiting Mars to search a large area around the intended landing site, but have found no sign of an impact crater, parachutes, airbags, or the lander itself.

This is a model of the *Viking 1* lander—a robotic probe that made a soft landing on the surface of Mars in 1976. It was a sophisticated robot that used a mechanical arm to collect soil, combine it with water and nutrients, then incubate the mixture in an effort to detect any microorganisms living in the soil. Although the robot performed its duties faithfully, scientists were unable to draw any firm conclusions from the results of the experiment.

other side of the planet in a larger, deeper crater and began sending back pictures. *Opportunity* appeared to be working perfectly.

From then on, things went more smoothly. The programmers at NASA restored full control of *Spirit* and were able to resume exploring. As this book is being written, *Spirit* has driven more than 3.5 kilometers (2.2 miles)—usually less than 10 meters (33 feet) at one go—and is now having to move backwards most of the time. That's because its right front wheel (it has six altogether) isn't working properly, and it's easier to steer the rover when it's dragging the damaged wheel behind it.

Opportunity has ventured down 15 vertical meters (50 feet) into Endurance Crater and studied several layers of bedrock. Both vehicles continue to operate more than six months after landing on the Martian surface—over twice their intended operating life. During that time the geologists have collected strong evidence that liquid water was present on the surface of Mars. The mission has been an unqualified success, thanks mainly to the durability and adaptability of these two remarkable robots.

Jake and Elwood

In 1912, the largest and most luxurious ocean liner ever built left Southampton, England, on its maiden voyage. The *Titanic* was scheduled to arrive in New York six days later. It never made it.

The ship, said to be unsinkable, struck an iceberg off the coast of Newfoundland. The collision ripped a long gash in its steel hull, opening five of its watertight compartments to the sea. Over the next three hours it took on so much water that it finally sank.

Titanic's builders had been so confident of their vessel's seaworthiness that they didn't include enough lifeboats for everyone aboard. Although the sea was glass calm that night, over 1,500 passengers and crew drowned in the icy water before rescue ships arrived.

The story of the *Titanic* is one of the most dramatic of modern times.

It's been told in hundreds of books and several films. The latest film, *Titanic*, earned more money than any other movie in history. Recently, its director, James Cameron, decided to make another movie about the sunken ship, this time a documentary.

Cameron wanted to get inside the wreck of the *Titanic*. Resting over three kilometers (two miles) down on the sea floor, it's far too deep for scuba diving, and manned submersibles are just too big to fit through the ship's passageways and hatches.

The only solution was to use robots.

Remotely Operated Vehicles have been used for years in underwater exploration, but even these were too large to suit Cameron. Being a very determined man with almost unlimited amounts of money, he asked his brother Michael, an engineer, to build a pair of robots small enough to travel freely through the sunken ship.

49

In this artist's drawing, *Spirit* prepares to examine a Martian rock. The instrument package the rover holds before it contains spectrometers (for telling what minerals the rock is made of) and a microscopic imager (for close study of the rock's crystal structure).

The result was Bot 1 and Bot 2, soon renamed Jake and Elwood by the crew. The robots are roughly cube-shaped and about the size of a microwave oven. Each contains a videocamera, lights, a battery, and maneuvering fans, and is attached to its parent manned submersible by a thin fiber-optic tether. This tether, reeled from a spool inside the robot, carries all the information between the robot and its mother sub.

Jake and Elwood's movements are controlled by joysticks. Cameron and his crew, hovering in submersibles over the wreck, were able to guide the robots through one of the larger openings to the interior. The grand wooden staircase was sucked out of the *Titanic* during its plunge to the bottom, leaving a large entrance hole leading to the lower decks.

Once inside, Jake and Elwood began their exploration of the ship's interior. They drifted through the corridors like ghosts. Everything their cameras captured inside was covered in a fine silt, and the robots' operators had to be careful not to stir it up with their maneuvering fans.

In one of the passenger cabins, the frame of a brass bed rose from the mud. There were no bodies or bones—they had long since decomposed. So had most of the clothing the passengers wore; all that was left was the occasional shoe. But on the remains of a dresser Jake found a bowler hat, looking as crisp and perfect as the day it was made. From a list of the passengers and the cabins they occupied, Cameron and his crew learned it belonged to a man named Henry Harper. He did not survive the sinking.

The *Titanic* was carrying some of the wealthiest people in the world, and all around the robots were the belongings of these first-class passengers. The poorer passengers were housed in the decks below, too far for Jake and Elwood's tethers to reach.

Hanging everywhere were rusticles, stalactites of iron oxide formed by bacteria feeding on the metal bulkheads. Eventually these bacteria will turn the *Titanic* into a layer of rust at the bottom of the ocean.

Their batteries running low, Jake and Elwood were retracing their path to leave the mighty ship when suddenly Elwood's battery failed. The motors driving its maneuvering fans died, and it floated to the ceiling of the dining room, dead in the water.

After a trip to the surface docked in the mother sub, Jake's batteries were recharged. The ROV was then returned to the dining room where Elwood was trapped. The plan was to attach a weight to Elwood using a patch of Velcro, with the hope that it would bring the trapped robot down from the ceiling. But after successfully attaching the weight, Jake accidentally cut its own tether—probably by dragging it over a sharp piece of metal.

Immediately the picture from its camera went dark. There was now no way to control the robot at all. The submersible crew could only watch, horrified, as Jake—and their only hope of rescuing Elwood—drifted out of the grand staircase and towards the surface. The chances of finding the tiny robot drifting in the open ocean were slim to none. Both robots would be lost.

Then one of the submersible's pilots noticed that Jake's severed tether had drifted very close to the submersible's manipulator arm. He grabbed the controls and used the sub's robotic hand to hook a claw over the tether. Then he began spinning the mechanical hand at the wrist, reeling in the tether like fishing line! It took over half an hour, but the pilot eventually dragged Jake back down to the submersible and was able to stuff it back into its garage with the sub's manipulator arms.

After another trip to the surface, Jake's tether was repaired and the robot again returned to the *Titanic* to

51

Spirit and *Opportunity* have been thousands of times farther from Earth than any human explorer, but for long-distance viewing they're amateurs compared with the Hubble Space Telescope. Even *Voyager* looks like a homebody by comparison. Although it has never left Earth's orbit, the Hubble has collected images from the edge of the universe, looking back in time billions of years. Remotely operated by scientists on Earth, it's one of the most successful robots of all time.

Sadly, the telescope is nearing the end of its useful life. The batteries and gyroscopes that align the semi-trailer–sized telescope will probably fail sometime in the year 2007.

A shuttle mission to Hubble to extend the telescope's life had been scheduled for 2006. But in 2003 the space shuttle *Columbia* burned up during re-entry to the atmosphere, killing all seven astronauts aboard. NASA decided that sending the shuttle to Hubble is too risky because the orbit leaves no possibility of reaching the International Space Station, which could serve as an orbiting refuge in an emergency.

Astronomers were understandably upset over the prospect of losing one of their greatest tools, but then a Canadian company, MDR Robotics, proposed sending their robot, Dextre, on a mission to extend Hubble's operating life another four years.

Dextre is an advanced, two-armed version of the Canadarm, the robotic arm the space shuttle uses. It looks almost like a stick-figure drawing of a man, with two arms extending from a central trunk. Dextre is designed to be operated in space by an astronaut sitting at a control console here on Earth.

Such a mission would not be easy. It took astronauts five or six separate spacewalks and some severe body contortions to carry out Hubble's last upgrade, in 2002. For a machine to perform similar tasks unaided would make it "the most complex robotic mission ever undertaken," according to Marc Garneau, the head of the Canadian Space Agency and a former shuttle astronaut himself. Replacing the gyroscopes is especially tricky.

A rescue mission would have three steps: the robot would have to find the telescope, then grab onto it, and finally perform the repairs. To replace the Hubble's wide-field camera, Dextre would have to pull out a module containing the instrument, then slide in the new camera. It's pretty much like pulling a drawer all the way out of a dresser and putting it back in—except that this is a very precise, tight-fitting drawer.

The Hubble Space Telescope orbits about 600 kilometers (370 miles) above the surface of the Earth. This photo was taken from the space shuttle *Discovery* as it approached the telescope on a servicing mission. The aperture door has opened in preparation for taking an image—just like taking the lens cap off a camera.

Dextre has some advantages over a human repair person, however. It can track precisely how it removed the old camera when pulling it out and exactly reverse its movements when putting in the new camera. It also has a sense of touch so that it knows exactly how much pressure it's putting on the part and if the drawer is starting to jam.

After completing its mission, Dextre would probably remain with the space telescope, and might even assist with any future problems that arise.

NASA originally insisted that sending a robotic mission to Hubble before it fails would be impossible. But they didn't count on the outcry from astronomers, the U.S. Congress, and the general public over the prospect of abandoning Hubble. After studying proposals for robotic repair missions from several companies, NASA finally gave Dextre the go-ahead in 2004, but later cancelled the mission. Now NASA's new chief administrator is reconsidering the decision. Dextre just wishes NASA would make up its mind.

rescue its trapped brother. This time it was equipped with a lance with a detachable hook and line on the end. Piloting Jake himself, Cameron charged at Elwood with the lance and stuck it through the mesh covering one of Elwood's maneuvering fans—like harpooning a seal!

Jake then towed Elwood back to the submersible, completing the rescue. A mission that could have ended in disaster was a success. Not only did these two little robots manage to save each other, but they gave the world a glimpse inside the most famous shipwreck of all time.

Autosub is hoisted out over a ship's deck in preparation for launch.

Dante I and II

The deep ocean and outer space are hostile environments, but at least conditions in those places are fairly easy to predict. An active volcano, by comparison, is a very danger-ous place because everything can change in an instant. That's why volcanologists (people who study volcanoes) are reluctant to go into them. In 1993, eight volcanologists were killed taking samples from two separate volcanoes.

Volcanology is the perfect job for a robot—or so thought the scientists from NASA and the Carnegie Mellon Institute who built Dante I and II. These tele-operated, eight-legged robots were designed to carry instruments into volcanic craters to take temperature readings and monitor the often deadly gases issuing from vents.

The scientists decided to test Dante I at Mount Erebus, an active volcano in Antarctica. After months of preparation, the intrepid robot walked about six meters (20 feet) into the crater before slipping and tumbling into the lava below. The scientists did not say whether it gathered any useful information on the way down.

The roboticists went back to the drawing board and come up with

Autosub

A true autonomous robot, Autosub-1 is used for marine exploration and guides itself by sonar and a technique called dead reckoning. In this method, computers calculate the sub's position in relation to its starting point by measuring how long and at what speed it has traveled in a certain direction. It is not under radio control, and finds its own way back to its origin point. Robotic submarines can cruise independently because open water has relatively few things to run into.

Autosub was built by the Southampton Oceanography Centre in England for marine research. It has no manipulator arms and looks essentially like a big torpedo. It can be fitted with a variety of instrument packages to perform different tasks—cameras for one mission, chemical sensors or thermometers for another.

During hundreds of successful dives, Autosub has done everything from mapping the underside of an Antarctic iceberg using sonar to surveying populations of krill (a finger-sized, shrimplike animal that lives by the billions in polar waters), to searching for minerals in Loch Ness.

Autosub has a maximum depth of around 1,000 meters (3,300 feet) and, curiously, is powered by

Autosub surfaces after a mission in polar waters. Robotic probes have one great advantage over human explorers: they can suffer much greater extremes of temperature, pressure, and radiation than an unprotected human body and still perform their tasks.

4,700 D batteries (presumably not included). It turns out that these household batteries are very efficient energy packages. Batteries with twice the power could have been custom-made for Autosub, but they would have cost 10 times as much.

In this daring story of human evolution, an alien space probe kick-starts the human race. The film opens in Africa several million years ago, a time before human beings have evolved. An upright, featureless black slab appears before a troupe of apes living on the edge of a desert. This is the Monolith, a robot sent by an advanced alien race to search the galaxy for intelligent life.

The Monolith examines the apes' minds and concludes that they have the capacity for intelligence. Then, somehow, it places the thought of using a bone as a weapon in the mind of one of the apes, prompting a primate to invent the first tool and start down the road of technology.

The film then jumps to 2001, a time when humans have bases on the moon. A team of astronauts investigating a strange magnetic field finds the Monolith buried 12 meters (40 feet) beneath the floor of a crater. Once uncovered, the Monolith sends a powerful burst of radio waves in the direction of the planet Jupiter.

Earth builds the spaceship *Discovery* to follow the radio burst, not knowing what it will find. Although there are humans aboard the spaceship, all of its functions are under the control of a single, super-intelligent computer named HAL—and so the spaceship is also, technically, an enormous robot.

HAL suffers a psychotic breakdown during the mission and kills all but one member of the crew.

When the Monolith reappears, the crew member is whisked across the galaxy to the aliens who have led humankind on this odyssey. There, he literally meets his maker.

Many critics have noted that compared to the robotic characters— HAL, the Monolith, and the *Discovery*— the human characters seem flat and uninteresting. The robots are truly the stars of *2001: A Space Odyssey*, still considered by many to be the greatest science-fiction film of all time.

Astronaut David Bowman leaves the spaceship *Discovery* in a smaller vessel known as a pod. Bowman is on a rescue mission to save a fellow astronaut who has been lured outside and murdered by the ship's computer.

Dante II, which had several improvements over its ill-fated predecessor. The most significant was that in addition to having legs, it had a winch that allowed it to rappel down steep slopes like a mountain climber with a rope around his waist. The winch line also served as the robot's *umbilical*. An umbilical is a bundle of cables that connects the robot to the people controlling it. It relays instructions to the robot and returns data from the robot's cameras and sensors. The lifeline also included a cable that supplied all of the robot's power.

But Dante II was not entirely dependent on this tether for guidance. While its operators, if need be, could control each of Dante's legs directly, when they wanted the robot to move quickly they could switch it to a semi-autonomous mode. In this state Dante could move much faster, accepting more general commands such as "Walk ahead 30 meters" or "Back up for the next 10 seconds."

Dante was equipped with a laser scanning system and cameras that allowed it to identify and skirt obstacles such as boulders or trenches. Around its body were sensors telling its computer brain whether it was upright or tilted and how much strain was on each leg or the winch cable. It was a very sophisticated robot.

Dante II's first field assignment was at Mount Spurr, an active volcano in Alaska. Project technicians set up a portable generator to supply Dante's power, as well as the satellite relay to send information from the robot to the scientists controlling it from a safe distance—over 100 kilometers (60 miles) from the active volcano.

Using its winch, Dante II rappelled down the steep crater wall to the floor of the volcano, a process that took about two days. The crater slope was covered in snow, ice, and ash. Boulders kept rolling down the slope. Several struck the robot, but it kept going.

Even under the best conditions Dante moves slowly, at about one centimeter (less than half an inch) per second, but the scientists kept accidentally guiding it into dead ends and boulders. It was hard to see with all the steam and smoke coming from the crater. Always the scientists were mindful of the tether, trying not to snag it on anything and making sure that Dante had a clear path back to the rim.

On the way down, Dante's seven cameras sent back clear pictures of conditions inside the volcano. Once on the crater floor, it spent three days collecting gas and water samples. It investigated many *fumaroles*, or volcanic vents. Then it came time to begin the climb out of the crater.

Early in the ascent Dante II lost

power, and for a while technicians feared the mission was over. They soon traced the problem to a short circuit in the power cable near the rim. An engineer was helicoptered to the volcano, the short circuit was fixed, and the robot resumed its ascent.

But there were more problems. Ash from the volcano had settled on the mirror used to aim Dante's laser scanner, and it could no longer be used for navigation. Instead, the scientists had to rely on video pictures to guide the robot. They kept turning Dante into dead ends, then having the robot descend back into the crater to try different exit routes.

Unfortunately, at about 60 meters (200 feet) above the floor Dante II lost its footing and rolled onto its side. The tele-operators were unable to get it back on its feet. Not wanting to lose their robot, or the samples it had gathered, they attempted a rescue. They removed the tether anchored at the rim of the crater and attached it to a helicopter. But the tether broke while the robot was suspended in midair, and it tumbled about halfway down the crater slope again.

Ultimately, two men had to hike down to the robot and attach a sling to it. The damaged robot was airlifted out of the crater, but its climbing days were over. In its golden years, Dante II toured North American science centers as part of a traveling display on robotics.

Many look upon the Dante expeditions as failures. Clearly, it was not the intent of the expeditions' funders to lose these expensive machines on their first missions. But as we have seen, there is always a price to be paid for exploration. Dante II collected important data from a very hostile environment, it taught NASA valuable lessons that were later applied to interplanetary robotic missions, and it did it all without the loss of human life.

And although the probes were lost, consider all of the unmanned probes we have sent to the moon and Mars. *Spirit* and *Opportunity* are not coming back to Earth— except perhaps as museum pieces in another hundred years—and their missions are considered triumphs of space exploration.

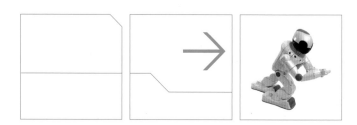

chapter 4

Fighting Robots

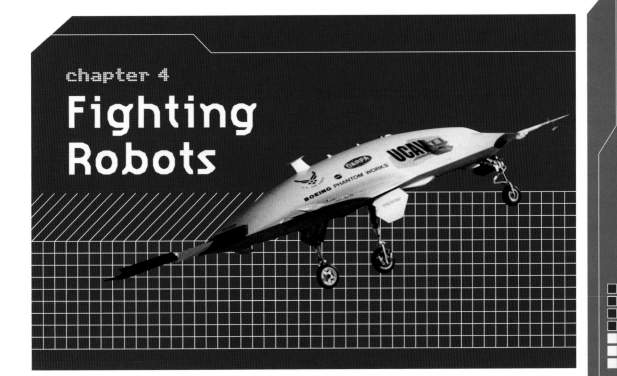

"A robot may not harm a human being or, through inaction, allow a human being to come to harm." Asimov's first law of robotics, written over 60 years ago, is still a solid foundation for the programming of intelligent robots. Sadly, no such program governs human behavior, and so we build robots for just the opposite purpose: to kill people. This is the ultimate aim of many military robots.

Currently, there are no robotic soldiers even on the drawing boards—at least nothing the Pentagon cares to talk about. Science is still decades away from producing effective humanoid robots like the battle droids of the

Star Wars movies. Even if such machines were possible, they would not be used as they were in those films. There's not much point in massing armies of robots on an open battlefield and having them fight it out with artillery and small arms when a single bomb from space could decide the outcome. Robotic soldiers would be useful for guerilla fighting from building to building in cities. They would require many of the same skills as robot butlers or maids: the ability to navigate doorways, stairs, and around furniture—all the features of buildings designed for human beings.

Still, military organizations around the world are working hard

Boilerplate was the invention of Professor Archibald Campion, who hoped "to resolve the conflicts of nations without the deaths of men." The idea was to fight a war with mechanical soldiers and so avoid the loss of human life—at least, human life on the side of whoever has the robots.

In 1888 Campion constructed a small laboratory in a space he rented in Chicago. He was hardly seen outside of it for almost five years, when he emerged to unveil his invention at the Chicago World's Fair of 1893.

Boilerplate was about a head taller than most men and had a torso shaped more like a household water heater. Permanently affixed to his head was an old-fashioned war helmet.

To demonstrate his abilities, Boilerplate participated in military campaigns all over the world, including the Spanish-American War, in which he led the charge up San Juan Hill. He also fought in the Russo-Japanese War.

During the First World War, Boilerplate vanished without a trace while fighting in northern France. It is believed he was either hit by an artillery shell or captured and dismantled by German forces, who studied the robot's technology to advance their rapid military buildup prior to the Second World War.

So given Boilerplate's success, why aren't all of the world's armies made up of metal soldiers? Because Professor Archibald Campion never really existed and neither did his invention, Boilerplate. They live primarily on the pages of a website: www.bigredhair.com. Anyone familiar with robotics would know that the technology to make Boilerplate doesn't even exist today, let alone 100 years ago. Still, that didn't stop tens of thousands of web surfers from being fooled.

The hoax was made more believable by convincing pictures that show Boilerplate standing next to real historic figures such as Teddy Roosevelt and Pancho Villa. The pictures were created using an image-editing program, combining photos of a scale model with archival photographs of the legendary figures.

Most people believe the science of robotics to be far in advance of its actual state. So when comic-book artist Paul Guinan sculpted a model of Boilerplate, took its photograph, and then inserted its likeness into photographs of historical figures, many web surfers believed that a mechanical soldier had actually fought in the Spanish-American War and later saved the life of Mexican revolutionary leader Pancho Villa, who stands next to Boilerplate in this photo.

to build robots; it's just that their inventions don't look anything like people. Instead, they take the forms of self-guided planes, tanks, and bombs. The U.S. military plans to replace one-third of its land vehicles with robotic vehicles by the year 2015. They're already experimenting with—and using—a wide variety of designs.

Robot Race

In the spring of 2004, DARPA—the Defense Advanced Research Projects Agency of the United States Department of Defense—held a competition to build a robotic vehicle capable of independent navigation. The rules were simple: the first to complete a course through the Mojave Desert on its own would be declared the winner. It would also win a $1,000,000 prize. Any vehicle entering the race had to be truly independent, navigating the course without human help after starting. It was allowed only one remote control: a kill switch. Of course, flipping the switch before the vehicle finished the course would mean losing the million dollars.

The contest drew 106 applicants. Most of the vehicles were guided by a combination of GPS (the American military's Global Positioning System) and some kind of video-aided navigation. These were often supplemented by radar, sonar, or laser beams to keep the robot on the road. Eventually, DARPA narrowed the applicants down to 15 entrants to begin the race in the desert just south of Barstow, California. Hopefully, at least one of them would end it in Pimm, Nevada. The entrants ranged from Carnegie Mellon University's renowned robotics lab to a group of students from a high school without so much as an auto shop.

At the starting line was an impressive array of vehicles. The largest was a 16-ton, six-wheeled Oshkosh Army truck. The smallest was probably The Ghostrider—a dirt bike put together by nine Berkeley University engineering students. How could a motorcycle expect to finish the course without a rider? In a word, *gyroscopes*.

There were converted sports cars. A huge Humvee. A home-built caterpillar-tracked vehicle powered by six electric motors. There was even one amphibious entry— a six-wheeled ATV known as CajunBot. Admittedly, the chances of actually meeting any water in the Mojave Desert were minimal,

but better safe than sorry.

After years of tinkering and testing, it was finally time to drop the starting flag. Two hundred and twenty-eight kilometers (142 miles) away lay the finish line, and a million dollars in prize money.

It might as well have been on Mars. CajunBot traveled 30 meters (100 feet) before lodging itself against a concrete barricade. The huge Oshkosh Army truck ran well for almost a mile and then, inexplicably, started backing up. Its handlers hit the kill switch, but not before their vehicle had retreated half the distance it had traveled. The Palos Verdes high school students ran into exactly the same concrete barricade as CajunBot. A four-wheeled ATV made it 11 kilometers (6.8 miles) before running off the road. A converted Jeep Grand Cherokee had to be shut off before it could ram a tow truck parked near the starting line.

And Carnegie Mellon's mighty Humvee? It traveled 12 kilometers (7.4 miles) before grounding itself on a wall of dirt. Although the robot could go no farther, it continued to spin one wheel in the dirt with such persistence that the tire eventually caught fire.

Finally, The Ghostrider, the little motorcycle that nobody thought could possibly win, didn't. As soon as it was released, it keeled over and had to be wheeled off the course.

Team ENSCO's entry in the 2004 DARPA Grand Challenge was a modified ATV nicknamed David. It was one of the finalists selected to enter the robot race from Barstow, California, to Pimm, Nevada.

Sadly, David traveled only about 300 meters (330 yards) before running up an embankment and rolling over. The accident left the robot just over 227 kilometers (141 miles) shy of the finish line and the $1 million grand prize.

Of the 15 final entrants, 8 never left the starting line. The 7 that did traveled a grand total of just under 47 kilometers (29 miles).

The DARPA Grand Challenge was hardly the leap forward in robotics that the military had hoped for. Still, DARPA plans to stage the event again in another year or two with the hope that the contestants have learned from their mistakes. In the meantime, the military will be holding on to its million-dollar prize.

Gort, a robot, revives Klaatu, an alien ambassador, aboard their flying saucer. The woman in the background runs the boarding house where Klaatu stayed during his visit to planet Earth.

The Day the Earth Stood Still (1951)

A flying saucer decelerates from the depths of space, circles the Earth several times, and touches down in Washington, D.C., in a park near the Washington Monument. So begins the 1951 science-fiction classic *The Day the Earth Stood Still*.

Immediately, troops and artillery are dispatched from a nearby army base. Within moments of the arrival of the military, a figure wearing a silvery suit steps out onto a ramp that extends from beneath the craft's door. He is Klaatu, emissary from another world. He looks like an ordinary 30-year-old white man.

Klaatu makes a brief speech welcoming the Earth to a galactic confederation of planets, but a nervous young soldier shoots and wounds him after mistaking the gift he presents for a weapon. Suddenly a second, much larger figure appears. This is Gort, a 2.5-meter-tall (eight-foot) robot. Gort's visor lifts, revealing not eyes but a dark space. A ray leaps forth, striking the soldiers' rifles, a tank, and several pieces of field artillery. The weapons dissolve in a blaze of light, but the soldiers are spared. Klaatu orders Gort to stop his attack, but we soon learn that it is Gort who is really in charge.

To eliminate war and violent crime, Klaatu's civilization has created a police force of robots and given them absolute mastery over all their worlds. These robots follow a simple program: if they witness any violent act, they immediately destroy the attacker. As a result, war and violence have vanished from this advanced civilization. Klaatu makes it clear that the robots' power cannot be revoked.

Klaatu and Gort have come to Earth with an offer and a warning: we may either join this peaceful society or, if we continue our violent and warlike ways, be destroyed by it.

More than half a century after it was made, this black-and-white film still looks convincing, thanks mainly to the superb design of both the spaceship and the frightening robot. Although Gort's shape is basically human, it has no eyes or mouth, and answers only to its own unalterable program.

The movie's producer, Julian Blaustein, was most troubled by the robot's knees, which he thought looked phony because the legs simply buckled whenever the actor inside took a step. To Blaustein it was obvious that it was just a rubber suit. But when the film was released, audiences simply accepted that Gort was formed of some advanced metal that could bend and then resume its original shape.

Until machine intelligence matures, telerobots are going to have to do the robotic grunt work. Already, remotely operated vehicles are performing some of soldiers' most dangerous jobs.

Gladiator is the nickname for the U.S. Army's Tactical Unmanned Ground Vehicle. Essentially, it's a small, remotely operated tank about the size of two kitchen ranges pushed together. At nearly the weight of a compact car, it's surprisingly heavy. Some versions of the Gladiator have six wheels, others caterpillar treads. The platform can carry cameras, instruments to detect dangerous chemicals, machine guns, and launchers for grenades, tear gas, or smoke bombs.

Gladiator can be used to clear a path through a minefield or draw fire from a sniper, revealing his location. The weapons, aimed by remote control, can also return fire. The remote control that guides Gladiator weighs about 9 kilograms (20 pounds) and can fit in a soldier's backpack.

Gladiator's purpose is to save human lives, both civilian and military. Obviously, a soldier's life may be spared if Gladiator is sent into a dangerous situation in his place. But using Gladiator can also save civilian lives. If, for example,

soldiers are sent into the midst of a riot for crowd control, they may end up having to fire on civilians to save themselves. But if Gladiator were sent into such a situation, even if its tear gas launchers failed to disperse a crowd who then turned upon it, the machine could always be sacrificed. Although expensive at $150,000, it's still just a machine. As one officer in charge of deploying the robot put it, "If they blow it up, they blow it up. At least we don't have to send any letters to its relatives."

There are many other telerobots operating in the U.S. military. Packbot, built by the iRobot corporation, was one model among dozens used in the wars in Afghanistan and Iraq, where they explored tunnels and caves in which enemy soldiers were hiding. Packbot is much smaller than Gladiator, weighing only 19 kilograms (42 pounds). It runs on caterpillar treads. Projecting from the forward drive wheels is a second set of tracks that allows the robot to climb stairs or other obstacles. It also has a manipulator arm for triggering or removing booby traps. Despite its light weight, Packbot is rugged. Soldiers sometimes get the robot into position by throwing it through a window or over a fence.

In April 2004, a Packbot in Iraq

became the first robot destroyed in combat. Most likely it was blown up while disarming a booby trap, but neither iRobot nor the army will say exactly what happened. Understandably, they're reluctant to reveal any of the robot's vulnerabilities.

Soldiers love the robots because the machines can do their most dangerous jobs for them. Prior to Packbot, a soldier clearing a cave of booby traps or mines crawled in with a grappling hook—a big metal claw attached to his waist by a rope. He would throw the hook out ahead of him and then drag it back in, tripping any mines it passed over. Not surprisingly, there weren't many volunteers for this job.

When an iRobot engineer was sent to the field to ask soldiers for suggestions for design improvements, their main criticism—apart from there not being enough of the robots—was that they were too big and heavy. They challenged the engineer to jog a mile carrying one of his robots in a backpack, and the

Robots were used extensively by the U.S. Army during its invasion of Iraq in 2003. Here, an ordnance disposal technician somewhere in Baghdad uses a remote control to send a Packbot in search of booby traps.

The U.S. Army is pursuing a more practical goal than a Boilerplate: communications and video technology that enhances the capabilities of human soldiers. The Objective Force Warrior will be a live soldier with electronic gear built into his clothing and weaponry.

Special Operations forces are already in constant communication with commanding officers through radio headsets. Their vision is enhanced by night-vision goggles and infrared gun scopes. The Objective Force Warrior will take these enhancements a step further. Suppose he has to enter a building occupied by enemy soldiers. A computer in his backpack will download satellite information and superimpose a map of the building on his helmet visor so the soldier will not have to pull out blueprints. The display might also show the locations of other squad members or even enemy soldiers.

Videocameras in his helmet will relay pictures back to officers in his command post or to a helicopter pilot.

The soldier's armor will be bulletproof. Sensors woven into his underwear will monitor his body's vital signs— heart rate, blood pressure, and body temperature. Air conditioning built into his clothing will cool or warm him, so

A mannequin models a prototype of the Objective Force Warrior system.

that he does not have to carry a bulky backpack full of clothing. There may even be built-in tourniquets that will automatically tighten if the soldier is wounded, restricting blood flow to the injured (or missing) limb until he gets medical attention.

If they had the technology, governments would undoubtedly build robot soldiers—machines to obey their commands without question, fear, or hesitation. But currently, no robot can match the abilities of the human body and brain combined. The best that scientists might be able to create in the foreseeable future is a cyborg—a melding of man and machine.

But as such a being evolves, we will have to ask ourselves some disturbing questions. Beyond what point are we no longer using machines to enhance human abilities, and instead using human beings as machine parts?

engineer went home convinced the soldiers were right. The problem is that as tracked and wheeled robots get smaller, they have more and more trouble crawling over obstacles, so there is a limit to how small they can be. Soldiers also asked that the robot's camera be mounted on some kind of flexible "neck," so that it could peer around corners. iRobot engineers are working on both problems.

There are much larger and faster telerobots on the drawing boards. Spinner is about the size of a Humvee, but because there's no one inside the vehicle, there is no need for windows or a passenger cabin. Each of its six wheels is driven by its own electric motor. Power for the motors comes from a turbine engine, just as in a modern train locomotive. If switched to battery power, the vehicle operates with very little sound. The air intakes and exhaust for the turbine can be sealed, so the whole vehicle can even run underwater.

Like Gladiator and Packbot, Spinner is tele-operated. A real problem with robotic vehicles is that they crash into objects far more often than vehicles piloted by a driver. These accidents often result in the vehicle flipping over, which could easily end the mission.

Spinner's designers have taken a very clever approach to the problem of the robot turning over: they just let it happen. If running over a boulder or into a ditch causes Spinner to flip, leaving it like a dead bug with its six wheels sticking up in the air, it simply shifts the wheels from what used to be the undersurface of the vehicle to the new undersurface; the top becomes the bottom and the bottom becomes the top. Then Spinner continues on its way. Such a strategy would be very unsettling for a driver, but Spinner doesn't have one.

Spinner can carry up to $2\frac{1}{2}$ tons of food, weapons, fuel, or anything else to supply troops. The interior cargo compartment can roll so the contents stay upright even if the entire vehicle turns over.

The more conventional way to deal with robot collisions is to avoid them in the first place. PerceptOR is a flying eye—a camera mounted on a small unmanned helicopter—that flies above and ahead of a ground vehicle. The helicopter and the ground vehicle are in constant communication. When the flying eye detects an obstacle such as a cliff or an enemy tank, it relays the information to the ground vehicle, which then steers around the trouble. The helicopter alters its course so that it always stays ahead of the vehicle.

The ground vehicle isn't completely blind; a camera is mounted on it, too. By combining the images from the two cameras, computers on board the ground vehicle can build up a much better view of the terrain.

Unmanned Aerial Vehicles

As the DARPA Grand Challenge demonstrated, just keeping a robot on the road is still not easy. But pilots don't have to contend with roads, and most of the time they only have to worry about colliding with one object—the ground. As a result, flying robots have been far more successful than their earthbound cousins. Remote-controlled planes were once called drones but are now referred to as UAVs—Unmanned Aerial Vehicles. Nobody loves acronyms more than the military.

Unmanned Aerial Vehicles are nothing new. Model airplanes were in the air before the Wright brothers made their first flight. Primitive drones saw combat as early as the 1960s. During the Gulf War of the early 1990s, Pioneer drones undertook 330 reconnaissance flights. Only one of these UAVs was shot down. These propeller-driven UAVs are quite small—about the size of a big model airplane. They were usually launched from catapults or with the help of rockets, and "landed" by flying into a net.

Today the Predator is the UAV most commonly flown by the U.S. Air Force. It's an odd-looking airplane with its long, thin wings

At an air force base in Iraq, a soldier adjusts the camera on a Desert Hawk UAV. Desert Hawks can be quickly launched by hand to scout the surrounding area for enemy troops or vehicles.

and bulbous nose. Without a pilot or crew, there's no need for windows, and because its V-shaped tail opens downwards, it looks a little as if it's flying upside down. Unlike the Pioneer, it can take off and land under its own power, and in between it can stay in the air for up to 40 hours. It's used mainly to take video pictures from cameras housed inside a globe hanging beneath the plane. Some of these cameras have such high resolution that they can spot a person up to 90 kilometers (56 miles) away. Others, using radar waves, can see through clouds, leaves, and sometimes even roofs!

The images captured by Predator may be used to help military commanders identify targets. Then the UAV can shine a spot of laser light on a target to draw laser-guided bombs or missiles from fighter jets to their destination. Finally, the Predator's cameras confirm whether or not the bombs have hit their target. All this time, the pilot remains safe on the ground, viewing the world from the Predator's cameras while operating the plane with a joystick. But this is no game—a point made very clear if you're on the receiving end of all this technology.

This animated movie set in 1957 tells the tale of a six-story-tall robot that falls to Earth from outer space. A dent in the robot's head has affected its memory, so it can't remember its purpose or origin. It knows only that it is grateful to Hogarth Hughes, who manages to shut off the power after the robot blunders into high-tension wires in the woods behind the boy's house.

Most of the film's comedy comes from Hogarth's efforts to conceal the giant robot from his mother, a snooping government agent, and everyone else in the small town where he lives. That's not easy, especially as the robot can only refuel itself by eating metal. It's got a big appetite and keeps taking bites out of parked automobiles and the local railway line.

Of course, Hogarth's secret eventually comes out and the army is called to the scene to subdue the iron giant. But the robot, it turns out, has more than a few tricks up its metal sleeve. If it is threatened by a weapon, it transforms into the military model, equipped with death rays, missiles, and rocket propulsion. It's about to go on a rampage against the U.S. Army when Hogarth manages to calm it down.

The Iron Giant is worth seeing not because it broke any new ground—just the opposite, it's something of a throwback in both its style of animation and its story—but because it's a lot of fun and one of the few intentionally humorous films starring a robot.

Another UAV, the Raven, has a wingspan of only $1\frac{1}{2}$ meters ($4\frac{1}{2}$ feet) and weighs less than 2 kilograms ($4\frac{1}{2}$ pounds). It can be taken out of its carrying case and launched by hand on missions lasting up to 80 minutes.

The Global Hawk is an even more advanced UAV. It is jet powered and flies at twice the altitude of commercial airliners. It can stay in the air for up to 24 hours—not as long as the Predator, but because it flies so high it can survey a much larger area during that time.

Unmanned Aerial Vehicles have been used mostly for reconnaissance but can also be modified to carry missiles or bombs. UCAVs (Unmanned Combat Aerial Vehicles) are true robots, flying their missions entirely under computer control. With advanced programming, a UCAV can identify new targets from the air or take evasive actions against enemy aircraft.

The Boeing X-47 is such a machine. It can carry so-called smart bombs and missiles, and has a smooth shape that reflects or absorbs radar waves, making it very difficult for an enemy to detect. The X-47 will someday be used in much the same way that cruise missiles are used today: to destroy an enemy's anti-aircraft defenses. And because it can carry more than one bomb, it is capable of destroying multiple targets.

Anyone Need a Slightly Used Pilot?

Modern fighter pilots already resemble cyborgs. Crammed into their cockpits, they barely have to move even their heads. All the information they need about their own plane and their targets is projected onto the windshield in front of them. It's called a heads-up display.

The lower half of the pilot's body is sheathed in a flight suit. This is like a pair of coveralls that are inflated during maneuvers such as high-speed turns. Such maneuvers put a lot of force on the pilot's body—six or seven times his weight. A pilot may lose consciousness as the blood is forced to his legs and lower body, depriving the brain. Inflating the suit squeezes some of the blood back up into the pilot's head. A fighter pilot is literally in the grip of his airplane.

But a flight suit can only do so much. As aircraft technology advances, the human body is rapidly becoming the limiting factor in a fighter jet's ability to

This photo was taken during the maiden flight of the Boeing X-45a, a prototype unmanned combat air vehicle commissioned by the U.S. military to test the practicality of using drones as attack planes. The X-45a carries bombs and can just as easily be equipped with missiles or machine guns.

The cruise missile is a UCAV that is stuffed with explosives and makes only one flight. Its stubby wings span about 2½ meters (8½ feet), short compared to its 6-meter (20-foot) fuselage.

Cruise missiles take off from airplanes, ships, submarines, or ground-based launchers, propelled by a booster rocket. Once the missile is clear of the launching vehicle, the booster falls away and the wings, air intake, and tail unfold. A turbofan engine then takes over.

The missile cruises at a low speed—slower than most commercial jets. But what it lacks in speed, it makes up for in craftiness. Cruise missiles are very accurate because they're guided to their targets by four separate systems:

→ **IGS (Inertial Guidance System)** keeps track of the missile's position by measuring its acceleration internally.

→ **Tercom (Terrain Contour Matching)** compares radar images of the ground below with 3-D images stored in memory. If they don't match, the missile adjusts course until they do.

→ **GPS (Global Positioning System)** measures the time it takes for signals to reach 3 of the U.S. military's network of 24 satellites, thereby pinpointing its location on the globe.

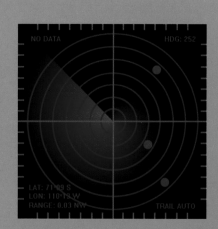

→ **DSMAC (Digital Scene Matching Area Correlation)** compares a camera image of the missile's quarry with one in its database so that it can zero in as it approaches final target.

By flying at low altitudes, hugging the terrain, cruise missiles avoid radar detection and are hard to hear coming. They strike without warning—and with deadly accuracy.

Cruise missiles launched from destroyers have been the first attack waves in the U.S. wars in the Persian Gulf, Afghanistan, and Iraq. These missiles destroyed anti-aircraft batteries, greatly reducing the risk to the crews of the bombers and fighter planes that followed them.

But some cruise missiles carry nuclear warheads, and each of these has the potential to kill millions of people. Unlike a conventional bomber with a human pilot aboard, there is no chance to recall a missile once it's on its way to a programmed target.

maneuver. With the UCAV, there is no pilot, and a plane that can make maneuvers placing 15 or 20 times the force of gravity on the aircraft might one day be built.

Modern fighter jets cost hundreds of millions of dollars each. Because UCAVs can be made so much more cheaply, can be operated without risk to a human pilot (because there isn't one), and will soon out-maneuver their piloted counterparts, some military planners believe that the latest generation of manned fighter planes is already the last. The dogfights of the future may well be fought entirely by UCAVs.

What's to Stop Us?

Past advances in the killing power of weaponry—chemical, biological, and nuclear—have encouraged generals and politicians to develop treaties that limit their use, and caused nations to agree to rules of warfare such as the Geneva Convention. Countries sign these treaties out of fear of what would happen to their own soldiers and civilians during a war.

Many historians argue that the development of nuclear weapons is all that has prevented a world war in the last fifty years. Since more than one nation acquired the atomic bomb, no one has dared use it, largely out of fear of retaliation.

The U.S. military now has an enormous lead in the development of robotic weaponry. The Pentagon assures the public that their goal is to save lives, and undoubtedly they have—American lives. Meanwhile, the gap in casualty figures between the United States and its enemies grows with each war.

But what if the generals achieve their goal and the day comes when we can enter into a battle without risk to our own troops? When machines do all our fighting, what will prevent us from resorting to war?

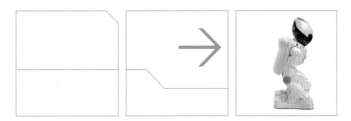

chapter 5
Working
Robots

By now you know something about the celebrities of the robot world, robots that have made headlines for setting a landing strut on Martian soil, for taking flak in the skies over the Persian Gulf, or for filling exhibition halls in 18th-century Paris.

That's all well and good, but someone has to clean up after these glory hogs. Who vacuums *Spirit* and *Opportunity*'s hotel room after the launch party? Who has to hold C-3PO's little golden hand when he catches a virus? And who unclogs the men's room toilet in the Hall of Presidents after Animatronic Abe uses one too many paper towels to clean himself up?

The working robots, that's who. Robots like Roomba and Pearl and MAKRO. Behind every prototype or one-of-a-kind robot are thousands of the mass-produced variety that are making their way into our factories, homes, and offices.

The majority of all the robots ever built toil away in darkened factories without a word of thanks, repeating the same tasks for weeks or months on end before being reprogrammed to do something else. The very first working industrial robot was Unimate, the arm anchored to the floor of a General Motors plant where it stacked parts it took from a mold.

Unimate may have been designed and first employed in the United

States, but it was Japan that welcomed the factory robot with open arms. It invested heavily in robotics research during the 1980s, partly because it was short of human workers and partly because Japanese firms plan much further ahead than many other multinational companies. Today, half of the world's one million factory robots work in Japan. The other half work mainly in the United States, Russia, Korea, Germany, Sweden, and Italy.

Robotic Co-workers

Forty-five years after Unimate, most industrial robots are still arms with tools called "end effectors" attached to the hand end. Their single most common job is the arc welding of car bodies. Most welding robots rely on precise placement of the parts to be joined. The robotic arm then moves to a predetermined place, clamps the two metal parts between its electrodes, and passes a very high-voltage current through them, fusing the parts.

A car built in this way is safer and stronger than one built by human welders. That's because a robot never misses any of the hundreds of welds that hold the body together. If it gets one car right, it gets them all right.

The assembly line of a modern automobile plant is an impressive sight, a ballet of swiftly moving mechanical arms with veils of sparks falling from the welds. It's also a very dangerous place to be, as almost all of these robots are blind. If you were to get in the way of one of them, it would simply continue going through its programmed movements, knocking you aside or worse.

There are industrial robots that can see—that is, their effectors are guided by cameras or lasers that measure distances precisely. For example, a robot that installs sunroofs on cars can find both the edges of the door and the edges of the opening in the roof and align them. Robotic vision is also used to guide electrodes and inspect welds on automobile bodies.

The main advantage of using robotic vision to guide tools is that the robot's precision doesn't deteriorate over time. The place where a blind robotic arm has been programmed to set tools or parts will gradually shift as moving parts in the arm wear down. But in a laser- or camera-guided robot, as the arm wears, it just moves a little more or less until the camera "sees" that the pieces are correctly aligned.

Robotic vision is also used in the

assembly of electronic appliances—DVD players, televisions, amplifiers, and more. Cameras guide the microchips or other components into position before robots use suction disks or pincers to plug them into circuit boards. Other robots use laser scanners and cameras to ensure that circuit boards are truly flat. If a part isn't up to standard, it is rejected before it ever becomes part of the product.

Finally, robots use cameras to inspect a completed assembly. The robotic camera is first shown an example of a product that has passed a careful visual inspection by a person. It snaps a picture of this object and stores it in memory. If the robot detects a significant difference between the image in its memory and an object on the assembly line, it halts the line or signals another robot to discard the flawed item. It's the sort of job that is perfect for a machine: it never dozes off and misses a faulty component or rejects a good one because it's having a bad day.

Robotic carts—called AGVs, or automatic guided vehicles—carry parts from place to place on assembly lines and in warehouses. Most are guided by wires buried in the factory floor. AGVs keep track of their position by counting wheel rotations, sensing magnets in the floor, or bouncing laser beams from reflectors mounted on the walls or shelves around them. Some of these carts can also load or unload themselves using forklifts. A system like this carries giant rolls of newsprint from the warehouse to the printing presses at some newspapers.

Robots have been a great success in factories and warehouses because these places are designed to accommodate them. In a factory, it's up to the people to stay out of the way of the machines. But what about other places of work?

A few robots have found their way into offices. The most successful is probably the Bell and Howell Mailmobile. This robotic letter carrier travels from office to office following a line painted on the floor. The line is only visible under ultraviolet light. Mailmobile follows the line through a building, stopping at each office long enough for a person working there to pick up her mail or to drop packages or letters in a fellow office worker's box. About 3,000 Mailmobiles have been sold since the late 1970s, and many are still in operation, but today their jobs have largely been replaced by e-mail. Even a robot can lose its job to automation.

Pearl is a prototype robot designed specifically for care of the elderly. This photograph features only Pearl's head, which is mounted on a wheeled, electric walker. Like many robots designed to work closely with people who are not technicians, Pearl has been given facial features in the belief that it will make talking or listening to the machine easier.

Robodoc

What's the last job you would think could be done by a robot? Many people would guess nurse or doctor—caring professions that require intimate human contact. But there is also a worldwide shortage of workers in these very professions, and nurses and doctors never have enough time. Robots are just starting to find their way into hospitals and nursing homes to provide some relief to these over-worked professionals.

Helpmate is another automatic cart, about the size of a washing machine. More advanced than Mailmobile, Helpmate can be sent directly to any room in the hospital without following tracks or wires. It navigates using a combination of cameras and sonar emitters, and has turn signals to warn people which way it's going next. Some models can even call elevators and travel between floors. Like the Mailmobile, it serves mainly as a courier, delivering meal trays, documents, drugs— just about anything that will fit in its carrying compartments and save a nurse or an orderly a trip.

Still in the early stages of development is Pearl, a robotic assistant for the elderly being developed by four universities in the United States, including the famous Carnegie Mellon Robotics Institute. Right now, Pearl is little more than a walker that can map out a nursing home's corridors using sonar. Rather than just go where an elderly person

Remember that scene in *Spiderman 2* in which a surgical team tries to remove a set of malicious mechanical arms from Dr. Octopus's back? The arms attack the nurses and doctors, tossing them around the room like rag dolls. Well, surgeons can now turn the tables on their evil-genius patients—and anyone else in need of an operation—with their own set of mechanical arms. Unlike Doc Ock 's arms, these don't have minds of their own, but with a surgeon's guidance they can perform the most delicate medical procedures.

There are several advantages to using remote-controlled, robotic instruments. They can move with great precision: a large movement of the surgeon's hand can translate into a much smaller movement of the instrument. Another advantage is that the instruments are held rock-steady. Even the best surgeon's hands may start to shake towards the end of an operation lasting several hours, but the computers controlling robotic surgical instruments can actually filter out hand tremors. Also, the surgeon can release the controls to rest his hands and the instruments will remain in place.

Perhaps the greatest advantage is that the incisions made during robotic surgery can be tiny—just large enough for a small camera and the surgical instruments to be inserted into the patient's body. To repair a heart defect, a patient's chest would ordinarily have to be cut open with a saw and the ribs spread apart to accommodate the surgeon's hands. But in 2002, surgeon Michael Agenziano used the DaVinci robotic system to perform heart surgery through just four small holes in the patient's body, each about a centimeter (less than half an inch) wide. He watched his instruments working on a special 3D monitor showing images from the surgical camera.

Doctors in New York have already used robotic tools to remove the gall bladder of a patient in France. Remote-control surgery could one day allow specialists to perform emergency operations on patients all over the world without arriving at a hospital exhausted and jet-lagged after hours of travel.

pushes it, Pearl can actually guide a patient from, say, the cafeteria to her room. It can also remind a patient when it's time to take his medicine or ask if he needs help from a human nurse. Pearl's makers hope that one day it will do far more. In the future it might have arms that would allow it to pick up objects or help a patient out of bed. Who knows, 40 years from now we may see ASIMO pushing one of these things around the Old Robots' Home.

After surgery, any good doctor will want to pay her patients a visit to see how they're doing. But if for some reason she can't make it to the hospital, a robot can help. At Johns Hopkins University hospital, a robot was recently used to make a surgeon's hospital rounds.

The robot stands a little shorter than the average woman and has a monitor for a head, a speaker for a mouth, and a videocamera for eyes. The doctor uses a joystick to move the robot (which rolls on three wheels) and adjust her view of the patient. The patient, in turn, sees an image of the doctor's face on the robot's monitor and can answer her questions by speaking into a microphone.

You might think that patients would be put off by having a robot visit them, but just over half of those involved in the trial said they preferred a tele-visit from their own physician to being examined in person by a doctor they didn't know.

Robots also work in medical testing labs, taking blood samples delivered from hospitals and doctors' offices, reading their barcode labels, and putting the samples in racks for the appropriate tests—many of which will also be done by robots. Others smear cells on petri dishes to culture them for medical research. Not only do laboratory robots save labor costs, but they do their jobs with absolute uniformity. This is vital to the accuracy of many lab tests and experiments.

As the baby boom generation ages and the proportion of elderly people in the Western world grows, the demand for medical services will rise steadily. More and more of those services will be provided by robots.

Remotely Operated Vehicles

Are there days when the only parts of your body to get any exercise are the thumb and forefinger you use to grasp a joystick? Are your parents constantly nagging you to get more fresh air and spend less time playing video games? Now you can tell them that you're training for a fulfilling career as an ROV driver.

You would think that the term

Endoscopy is the medical procedure of inserting a fiber-optic tube into the human gut to supply images to a camera. This means either going in through the mouth and down the throat or entering the digestive tract through what is politely called...the other end. Either way, it's no fun for a patient.

Doctors have now invented an alternative way of taking pictures inside the body. They've managed to put a tiny videocamera and a transmitter into a capsule about the size of a large vitamin pill. The patient swallows it and the pill travels through the digestive tract. When it enters the small intestine—an area almost impossible to reach with an endoscope—it starts transmitting pictures to a receiver the patient wears

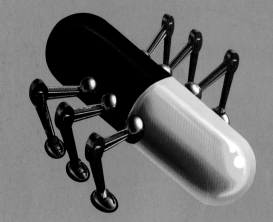

on a belt. The capsule has tiny light-emitting diodes that give off enough light for the camera to form images. The entire trip takes about eight hours, and a capsule can take up to 50,000 images—usually more than enough for a doctor to spot whatever is bothering the patient.

Is such a camera a robot? Not quite. A robot must be able to move under its own power. But scientists are working to attach tiny legs to the capsule so that it will one day be able to crawl through the intestine—even "upstream." The legs would have to fold up inside an outer capsule for swallowing. Once inside the intestine, the outer capsule would dissolve, allowing the legs to deploy—much like the landing gear on a space probe.

Engineers are looking at the use of *memory alloys*—metals that will deform, then resume their shape when heat or electric current is applied. The inner capsule could scuttle through the bowel right to diseased or injured tissues. Someday the robot might even have simple surgical instruments attached to it.

ROV would apply to any tele-robotic vehicle, but for some reason the name is usually given to robotic submarines and under-water tractors. Today, well over 3,000 of these telerobots are

working in the world's oceans, and all of them require human operators. The pilots sit aboard surface ships, watching monitors supplied with pictures from cameras on the ROVs. Computers convert the motions of joysticks, levers, and other controls into electronic signals that guide maneuvering fans and mechanical hands.

Many ROVs are used for laying and repairing cable in water too deep for divers. The growth of the Internet has caused a huge increase in the demand for submarine fiber-optic cable. Each year, enough new cable to circle the world four or five times is laid on the sea floor. If these cables aren't buried, they can be snagged and severed by ships dragging fishing gear or anchors.

To avoid these costly accidents, ROVs that are basically underwater tractors drive alongside the cable and dig a trench in the ocean bottom by squirting powerful jets of water into the sediment. Once the trench has been dug, another ROV uses a manipulator arm to drag the cable into the trench. Then the trench is filled in.

Free-floating ROVs carrying cameras are often used to look for breaks in cables or just to keep an eye on cable-laying operations. Because they don't move very quickly, streamlining isn't important and so unmanned submarines are often just tubular frames crammed with lights, cameras, manipulator arms, and maneuvering fans. Although they can withstand great pressure, what often limits how deep they can go is the length of their *umbilicals*—the bundles of

Although they worked long ago in a galaxy far, far away, R2-D2 and C-3PO are probably the world's most famous robots. C-3PO is a bumbling, golden, human-shaped protocol 'droid. His main skill is as a translator—although we rarely see him actually translating anything except for the beeping and chirping of his sidekick, R2-D2.

The trash-can–shaped R2-D2 understands English perfectly but can't speak it, which is why he needs C-3PO to make himself understood by human movie audiences and beings throughout the galaxy. R2-D2 can communicate with the computers controlling ships and other machines, and plugs into Luke Skywalker's X-wing fighter before every mission. He also serves as a courier, delivering holograms to other characters in the movie.

R2-D2 and C-3PO don't make much sense as robots. Given the advanced technology of their inventors, their jobs could easily be done by computers small enough to fit in an alien's pocket. But as dramatic characters they have won the hearts of millions of moviegoers. Between the two of them they provide most of the original *Star Wars* trilogy's funniest moments.

Like most movie robots, they are played by actors wearing extremely uncomfortable costumes. Yes, there is a very small man inside R2-D2. His name is Kenny Baker and he stands just 111 centimeters (3 feet 8 inches) tall.

83

MAKRO is a segmented robot designed to crawl through pipes in search of breaks or blockages. Looking for trouble spots in this way is far more efficient than the trial-and-error method of using heavy machines to dig up underground pipes—a costly and messy business.

cable that carry power and information between the ROV and its surface ship. With hundreds of meters of umbilical behind it, even a slow current will drag on the ROV with so much force that it's impossible to keep it in place.

Similar underwater robots are used by the oil and gas industry for laying and inspecting pipes or in the construction of deep-water oil rigs.

AUVs (Automated Underwater Vehicles) don't require an umbilical. These are true robots, moving entirely under the control of their computer brains. They are usually torpedo-shaped, and may take sonar surveys of the ocean floor or even swim with schools of fish, sending back video or other information to scientists.

Rotorobo

Then there are the jobs that people *could* do but would rather not. Take sewer-pipe inspection. If ever there were a job invented for a robot, this is it. One of the most advanced of these inspection robots is a German invention called MAKRO, a segmented robot that looks a little like a caterpillar. MAKRO has a pair of wheels supporting each of its six spherical segments and is about 2 meters (6 ½ feet) long. It's designed to inspect pipes from 30 to 60 centimeters (1 to 2 feet) in diameter.

MAKRO moves under internal computer control, and navigates by counting junctions with other pipes, manholes, and joints. Its head and tail segments have their own video-cameras and lights, giving engineers

Silent Running (1972)

This offbeat film was directed by Douglas Trumbull, responsible for the groundbreaking special effects of the film *2001: A Space Odyssey*.

In *Silent Running*, Lowell Freeman works aboard a space-going freighter in the distant future. He tends the forest growing at one end of the ship, its plants and animals the world's only surviving ecosystem. All natural habitats on Earth have been destroyed by pollution and war, so the forest is being maintained in space until Earth can be made habitable again.

Lowell cares so deeply about the forest that when he is ordered to abandon it and return to Earth, he instead jettisons his crewmates. He

is left with robots as his only companions—three short, waddling boxes with legs, named Drone 1, Drone 2, and Drone 3. Lowell grows increasingly fond of the drones and renames them Huey, Dewey, and Louie. We never learn exactly why he names the robots after Donald Duck's nephews, but it might have something to do with the robots' waddling gait.

Like R2-D2 of the *Star Wars* movies, Huey, Dewey, and Louie understand English perfectly but cannot speak themselves. They communicate with one another by movements of small vents in their heads—or rather, where their heads would be if they had them. Although they make almost no sound at all, these three robots are endearing characters. Their moods and personalities are expressed by the movement of their boxy bodies, and by Lowell's reactions to them.

The drones were operated by three amputees—actors who had lost their legs. They walked on their hands, which they inserted into the robots' feet. An adult with all of his limbs couldn't have fit inside the costume.

a good view inside the pipe. Mercifully, MAKRO has no sense of smell.

Electric motors drive the wheels but also control the joints between segments, so that MAKRO can rear up to climb over ledges or snake around corners. The robot has no arms or hands, so it can't really do anything to repair a leak when it finds one, but by pinpointing the location, it can save repair crews digging up hundreds of meters of pipe.

The Vanguard MK 2 comes with a videocamera, microphone, speakers, and a manipulator arm ending in a set of tongs. The tongs can operate anything from a car door handle to a conventional doorknob. The telerobot can also carry radiation detectors, chemical sniffers, and small water cannons called disruptors, which can disable a bomb without detonating it.

In Case of Emergency

Another job that nobody should have to do is bomb disposal, and bomb squads around the world use telerobots as their first line of defense. One of the most popular models is the Vanguard MK 2, made by a Canadian company. Essentially, it's a tractor with a videocamera and a grappling arm that can lift up to 16 kilograms (35 pounds). It's used to grab a bomb and carry it to a containment tub or a safe distance away from buildings and people, where it can then be detonated.

Although it's not as fast as bomb-disposal robots with wheels, the Vanguard's caterpillar treads enable it to climb stairs. It's small enough to fit in the trunk of a car or crawl underneath one to retrieve a bomb.

Vanguard is controlled using a standard laptop computer and a joystick. The U.S. military employed some 50 of the robots for bomb disposal during its campaign in Iraq. At $45,000 to $55,000 US each, they're considerably cheaper than their competitors. And of course, no one can put a price on the lives they may save.

Similar robots are used by fire departments to enter buildings where materials that give off hazardous fumes are burning. Their manipulator arms are usually adapted to carry fire extinguishers or hoses, and they have to withstand much higher temperatures than other telerobots. All of the hoses and wires—especially the umbilicals—must be sheathed in heat-resistant materials.

After the World Trade Center in New York collapsed following a terrorist attack in 2001, the grim search for survivors began. This was dirty and sometimes dangerous work. The gray dust that covered everything after the collapse made it very difficult to see survivors. The dust even plugged the rescue dogs' noses, so that it was hard for them to smell anything.

Within hours of the attack, engineering professor Robin Murphy and three of her graduate students were there with eight telerobots. The robots carried thermal cameras to detect body heat and microphones to listen for human voices. Other cameras were tuned to look for colors—particularly red.

The robots were not very successful. They were too large to fit between the chunks of concrete, and even where they could, the rubble was too coarse for the tracked vehicles to move through. Their tethers kept getting hung up in the debris.

But Murphy says that experiments with rescue robots will soon pay off. Human rescuers entering disaster areas often put themselves at great risk. The aftershocks of an earthquake can bring walls down on rescuers searching through the debris. But a sturdy enough robot could survive such a collapse.

The Tokyo Institute of Technology has developed a robot called Souryu, which means "blue dragon." The meter- (three-foot-) long robot has three segments, each of which has two sets of caterpillar treads. The treads are deeper and wider than the body segments they're attached to, so that even if Souryu rolls over, its tracks still make contact with the ground. Its snakelike shape is ideally suited to crawling through wreckage, where it could be used to locate survivors or drag a hose to supply drinking water until survivors can be dug out.

Souryu uses a radio antenna to relay information to and from a control console. A big problem with radio-controlled rescue robots is that if they crawl too far into the debris, the radio signal is blocked and they lose contact with their handlers. What is really needed is a robot smart enough to find its way in and out of the wreckage and then report its findings.

The Roomba, a robotic vacuum cleaner, is the world's largest-selling home robot. While it doesn't have the suction power of a conventional vacuum cleaner, it can increase the time between human-assisted vacuumings by removing unsightly dirt such as pet hair.

Cleaning Up

Cleaning things is a large part of the work done in the world every day. In North America alone, over 5 million workers are employed in cleaning commercial buildings—that's everything from vacuuming to emptying trash cans to cleaning toilets in offices, factories, stores, schools, and government buildings. Add to that the work done in private homes—most of it unpaid—and you have a huge labor force. And that doesn't include all the trains, cars, ships, airplanes, roads, and parks that need cleaning.

Right now, it's almost all done by people. Cleaning usually means running some kind of cloth or sponge over whatever is being cleaned, but machines have trouble dealing with irregular surfaces. And even with very flat surfaces like floors, they must first be cleared of obstacles, involving yet more manual labor. A few machines, such as dishwashers and power washers, get around the problem of irregular surfaces by using jets of water, but that's not going to work too well for your television set or those bookshelves in the den.

Robots are just beginning to get a handle on the job of cleaning, starting with the relatively easy tasks like vacuuming. There are now several models of robotic vacuum cleaners on the market. The best cost almost $1,800 and navigate by sonar. The most popular, largely because of its low price—it retails at around $200—is the Roomba, manufactured by the iRobot Corporation, one of whose founding members is Rodney Brooks—the man who, you may recall, is the father of Cog.

The exact rules, called *heuristics*, that determine the pattern Roomba uses to sweep a room are a trade secret, but the vacuum cleaner usually begins by spiraling outward from its starting point. When it eventually encounters a wall, it may either edge along it or gently bounce off in a random direction following a straight line. Other obstacles also cause it to move off in a random direction. iRobot claims that it first developed Roomba's heuristics for a minesweeping robot it was building for the army.

While it does work, Roomba is hardly the breakthrough in robotics that consumers have been waiting for. It's not very intelligent, doing little more than bumble from one obstacle to the next. But it has potential. Some owners use it as a platform for their own robotics experiments and modifications.

You can check it out at: www.roombacommunity.com.

In this science-fiction thriller set in the year 2035, Del Spooner is a police detective who despises the humanoid robots who work all around him, doing everything from walking dogs to cooking meals. These robots, which have beautiful, transparent bodies and animated faces capable of nearly human expression, were created largely without animatronics. Instead, they are computer-generated animations, moving with grace and speed.

The robotic characters are all kind, courteous, and physically superior to human beings. They are also bound by Asimov's three laws of robotics (see page 15).

And so, when Spooner is called to investigate a murder and concludes that a robot is guilty of the crime, no one believes him. No robot has ever harmed a human being and no robot ever could!

It's a classic mystery in the tradition of Isaac Asimov, although I, Robot is not actually based on any of his short stories. The script was written by a screenwriter named Jeff Vintar and sold to a movie studio in 1995. Later, that studio also acquired the rights to Isaac Asimov's short stories, and decided to combine Asimov's title and Vintar's script.

So can a robot programmed to protect human beings commit murder? It can if the murder is for the benefit of many other human beings. The solution to the mystery posed by I, Robot is quite clever, and examines the old question of whether or not it is wise to put so much work— and so much power—into the hands of our servants.

Detective Del Spooner (played by Will Smith) searches for Sonny, a rogue robot he suspects of murder. Sonny has chosen a great hiding spot—a room filled with thousands of robots that look just like him.

There, hobbyists can trade ideas and information about their pet projects, which include turning control of their Roomba over to a home computer, converting it into a toy turtle, or making it quieter.

If you're looking for a cleaning robot with a little more power, you might want to try the M3500. Of course, it won't be of much use unless you happen to own a freighter or naval destroyer in need of a paint job. Every few years large ships have to be put into dry dock to have their hulls repainted. The most time-consuming part is stripping off the old paint, a job that used to take dozens of workers several days.

The M3500 is a telerobot that can do the job in about half the time. It crawls over a ship's hull, peeling off the old paint with a jet of water at a pressure of over 380,000 kilopascals (55,000 pounds per square inch). It's also better for the environment than sandblasting because a vacuum sucks up the waste water and sends it down a hose to filters that remove the paint.

The robot rolls on wheels but is held against the ship by a powerful magnet. An operator uses a joystick to guide the robot over the hull.

Similar robots have been created for cleaning the windows of skyscrapers. The M-10, developed by roboticist Henry Seemann, uses six vacuum feet to hold the robot to the glass while drive wheels pull it along at about lawnmower speed. It cleans the windows with steam, then dries them with a jet of air. It's tele-operated, like the M3500, but later models will probably be able to find their way around a building on their own. The M-10 can also be adapted to sand down or spray-paint aircraft.

Over the next decade such highly specialized robots will become more common outside factories, replacing people doing skilled but repetitious work. Although each will be able to do only one job, it will have some ability to adapt to its surroundings.

What roboticists are working towards is the universal robot—a machine in the basic form of a human being and almost as versatile. It will have arms and legs and eyes and be able to understand verbal commands. Such robots are still decades away, but in the meantime, specialized robots will begin to relieve their human masters of jobs one at a time.

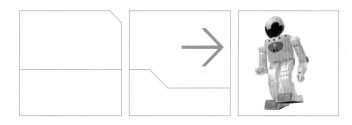

chapter 6

Robots at Play

We've been pretty hard on the robots. We've handed them our worst jobs. We've prodded them to fetch and walk and speak. We've told them how to think, with dismal results. We've got this notion in our heads that we can create a machine in our own image, and can't seem to let it go. And when the odd robot finally does perform beyond expectations, how do we respond? With pitchforks and flaming torches. It's hardly worth getting up off the slab in the morning.

So in this chapter we'll give robots a break—a little time off to play—because one thing robots have never failed to do is entertain us. In movies, television shows, science fairs, and theme parks, they thrill millions of people every year. And as toys, they never go out of style. In fact, they're more popular than ever.

Why have robots been so successful in the arena of play? Partly it's because our expectations are more relaxed. There is simply less at stake with toys. If a robot warrior designed to crush its competitors ends up in pieces instead, we're likely to say that's just part of the game: there are winners and losers. We might even laugh. If, on the other hand, an airliner on autopilot miscalculates its altitude on landing, the mood on the tarmac will be less than merry.

Strictly for Show

So what do robots do for fun? Put on a puppet show. That's really all that animatronics is—a powered puppet show. The original term, coined by the Disney Corporation back in the 1960s, was *Audio Animatronics*. They invented the technology for puppets powered by air pressure in the Enchanted Tiki Room in 1963. In the exhibit, dozens of mechanical birds would open and close their beaks, lift their wings, or swivel on their perches in time to music and sound effects.

The show was an impressive technological feat for the time. Tones recorded on reels of magnetic tape initiated the birds' every movement by causing metal reeds inside the birds to vibrate. The reeds in turn activated pneumatic valves. Technically, the puppets qualified as robots because they could have been reprogrammed to move in different sequences—although recording all the tones onto master tapes was such a time-consuming process that it never happened. Years later, control of the exhibit was switched over to computers.

Disney's next milestone was an animatronic Abraham Lincoln, originally created as a temporary exhibit for the 1964 World's Fair. It was powered exclusively by hydraulics. Pneumatics had been

well suited to the Tiki birds with their quick, sharp movements, but hydraulics produce smoother, more lifelike movements for larger figures.

The animatronic Lincoln's movements were so realistic that while he was still just a head on the bench at Disney, he frightened a janitor so badly that he refused to return to work the next day. After their success with Lincoln, Disney concentrated on hydraulically powered figures, and for years their exhibits were at the forefront of animatronics.

Maybe not the most lifelike animatronic figure, but certainly among the most memorable, is the mechanical shark used in the 1975 movie *Jaws*—a tele-operated robot. Affectionately known as Bruce by the movie's cast and crew, it had only been tested in fresh water before it was brought to the movie set. The moment the shark was lowered into salt water, it shorted out and had to be rewired. It never did work particularly well, and the results were less than convincing. Luckily, most of Bruce's rather stiff body remains underwater for the bulk of the film. All we see is the dorsal fin and the curiously immobile upper lobe of the tail, knifing through the water. Only when Bruce breaks the surface for a snack do we see the bloody

93

←

Bruce the mechanical shark entertains visitors on the Jaws ride at the Universal Studios theme park. Dozens of times each day, Bruce terrorizes boatloads of tourists, and always he meets a tragic end: here he's seen chomping on a high-voltage underwater cable and electrocuting himself.

mouth and the rows of rubber-sharp teeth.

In the 1990s, the animatronic shark was recreated as part of the Universal Studios tour. A few years later, it was completely rebuilt and has been a great success. The tour takes its first wrong turn when participants come across the wreckage of the previous tour boat, which includes a floating set of Mickey Mouse ears. Through the ride, Bruce keeps lunging out of the water to the delight of shrieking tourists. Of course, Bruce is really several Bruces, each lurking below the surface at a different point and capable of just one movement.

The animatronic figures that partake in these rides, while complex, are not really robots. They perform the same sequence of movements over and over, much like the tropical birds of the Tiki Room.

Today, the real animatronic stars perform in movies, and these are all telerobots. The largest of these actors is the Spinosaurus that appeared in the movie *Jurassic Park III*. It's over 13 meters (45 feet) from snout to tail—roughly the size of a real Spinosaurus—and weighs almost 11,000 kilograms (24,000 pounds). The skin is made of foam rubber and most of the robot's movements are powered by hydraulic pistons. It's all hung on a frame made of carbon fiber and steel.

It takes eight puppeteers to operate the Spinosaurus, each controlling a different part of the body. There's one operator for the head, two for the main body, one for the tongue, another for the eyes, one for the tail, and another still for a bladder inside the chest that simulates the dinosaur's breathing. The robot's arms are controlled by a special harness that the eighth operator puts on over his own shoulders, arms, and hands. As the puppeteer moves, the harness transmits radio signals to receivers inside the robot. Computers then activate the hydraulics and the puppet duplicates the operator's arm motions.

The Spinosaurus puppet is extremely powerful. Its hydraulics generate nearly 745 kilowatts (1,000 horsepower), giving it the strength to tear a car apart.

Of course, for sheer car-crushing power Spinosaurus must take a back seat to Robosaurus, billed as the world's largest entertainment robot. Robosaurus has the basic shape of a *Tyrannosaurus rex* on wheels. Standing as tall as a five-story building, weighing over 27,000 kilograms (60,000 pounds), and breathing jets of fire, Robosaurus can be rented by anyone willing to pay $25,000 a day—and able to provide a large area free of breakable objects.

In addition to destroying cars, Robosaurus has a résumé (at www.robosaurus.com) that really speaks for itself (Robosaurus can also supply letters of recommendation on request). Here are a few highlights:

- crushes cars with 11,000 kilograms (24,000 pounds) of gripping force
- bites and rips out roofs and doors using stainless steel teeth
- throws the mangled morsels to the ground
- transforms into a legal, licensed trailer for transportation across the nation's highways
- sleeps on the road between performances, resting its head on the tractor's fifth-wheel plate like a pillow

The only person having more fun than the loyal fans who crowd sports stadiums around North America to see the robot perform is its operator, who gets to ride inside the mechanical dinosaur's head!

Robot vs. Robot

Nothing draws a crowd like a fight—even when the combatants are robots. The idea of pitting robots against one another as a spectator sport began in the early 1990s with Marc Thorpe, an employee of Industrial Light and Magic, the company started by director George Lucas to create the special effects for *Star Wars*. Thorpe tried building radio-controlled appliances that he hoped would help him with boring chores like vacuuming and ironing. They didn't work too well.

As often happens with thwarted geniuses, Thorpe turned his powers towards evil. He attached power tools and chainsaws to the mobile platforms he had originally designed to do housework. Urging some of his friends to do likewise, he staged the first robotic battle before an audience in San Francisco. Thorpe joined forces with a small record company to promote the event, and its popularity grew. Without Thorpe's permission the record company showed video of the event to a producer who took the idea to BBC television in England. The BBC produced the television series *Robot Wars,* broadcasting the first episode in 1998.

The idea of *Robot Wars* is simple: place two or more radio-controlled robots in an arena and turn them loose on each other. The object of the game is to destroy or immobilize your opponent. The last robot left moving is the winner.

The robots are radio-controlled by the teams that design them, and compete within one of several weight classes, up to 200 kilograms (441 pounds). Some of the robots use hammers to pound their enemies into submission. Buzz saws are also popular weapons. Others use forklift-like devices to overturn their opponents. Just about any kind of weapon is allowed as long as it does not employ fire, explosives, or radio jamming. Weapons that deliver an electric shock, such as Tasers, are also prohibited. Pits and other traps built into the floor of the arena wait to bake, chop, or crush the contestants.

The show was extremely popular, running for seven seasons. It was canceled in 2004, but robotic combat sports continue in live events. Around the world, hundreds of teams— usually consisting of four or five male nerds with a flair for mechanics, computer programming, or electronics—devote much of their spare time to their mechanical gladiators before sending them off to almost certain destruction in the arena.

Sometimes there are prizes for the winners, but most teams are in it for the glory. And as for the audiences, they get to experience the thrill of destruction while knowing that no one is actually being hurt—except for some dented pride, that is.

For the Rest of Us

What if you want your own robot but simply don't have the mechanical skills of a special-effects technician like Marc Thorpe? For the rest of us, there are toys. True robots make great toys because they can be reprogrammed to do different things, greatly increasing their play

RoboCup

If you were designing a team sport for robots, you'd probably start with a relatively simple game—like soccer, whose basic rules are: put the ball between those two posts and don't use your hands. Officials for the Robot Soccer World Cup have simplified the rules even further: players *can* use hands, if they have them.

The goal of RoboCup is to stimulate development of artificial intelligence through robot soccer tournaments. One league plays with an orange golf ball on a field the size of a Ping-Pong table. Another calls for a cantaloupe-sized ball and a field about a third the size of a basketball court. Still another specifies that the players must be humanoid robots. There's even a league for modified AIBOs—the Sony company's robotic toy dog (see page 104).

Teams may consist of anywhere from 1 to 11 players, but they must all be true (not tele-operated) robots under computer control. The computers are allowed to coach from the sidelines, however. Rules for the humanoid league are more relaxed, where it's really more of a demonstration sport than a tournament at this point.

Since the first RoboCup in 1997, hundreds of teams from over 37 nations have competed. As spectator events, the matches to date have been less than thrilling. Just finding the ball, let alone keeping it in play, is a challenge for most robots. More than one game has ended with both teams wandering off the field and getting lost. Still, RoboCup has set the ambitious goal of fielding a robot team capable of defeating the human world champions by the year 2050.

At the 2004 RoboCup championships in Lisbon, two robots scrap for possession of the ball in an event from the humanoid competition. As the name implies, contestants in this league must have the basic form of a human being—two legs, two arms, and a head.

value—the ability to amuse their owners over time.

The humanoid robot has long been a popular model for toys, but most of them have been wind-up or battery-powered devices that repeat, at best, a single series of motions. In the 1950s, Hasbro Toys sold Walkie Talkie, a simple telerobot that had the ability to roll along the floor and repeat a few recorded phrases. The remote control was connected to the robot by wires.

In 1969, it was again Hasbro that pushed toy robotics forward with a series of electric cars called the Amaze-A-Matics. The cars were powered by an electric motor that, in addition to driving the wheels, operated a pair of pinch rollers. The rollers would grab a program card inserted just beneath the front bumper and slowly feed it into the car's chassis. Indentations cut into the sides of the card nudged levers in and out. The lever bumping along the left side of the card controlled the car's steering; the lever on the right, the transmission. Depending on the depth of the indentations, the car would move forward, stop, or reverse while the front wheels turned left or right, or stayed straight. The car completed its maneuvers by spitting the card out the back bumper. Included in the box were several blank cards that the owner could trim to create custom programs.

The Amaze-A-Matics were a clever design—although probably not quite as amazing as the stunned expressions of the father and son depicted on the box would have you believe. The toys were marketed as "The Fantastic Car with a Brain!" It's an accurate enough description, provided you define the word *brain* as a strip of cardboard with some notches cut into the edges. Hasbro later sold a bizarre-looking tracked robot called Mr. Amaze-A-Matic that could be programmed by the same cards.

Between October 1998 and December 1999, Furby was the most loved and successful toy robot in history. During this period Tiger Electronics sold over 12 million of the fuzzy gremlins. Furbys looked like stuffed toys but were crammed with some sophisticated electronics. (If you'd like to see some of them, visit the Furby Autopsy website at http://www.phobe.com/ furby/index.html.) They could wiggle their ears, open and close their eyes, and even move their little beaked mouths while speaking. They had vocabularies of several hundred phrases, consisting of words from both the English and Furbish languages. If startled by a loud noise like a handclap, their eyes would fly open. When the light fell below a certain level, they would go to sleep.

On a more sinister note, Furbys

A.I. begins in the not so distant future and tells the story of David, a robot in the form of an 11-year-old boy. David is bought by a couple whose only son has been put into cold storage until a cure can be found for his terminal illness. The chances that he will ever be revived are slight.

Shortly after David is purchased, his adoptive parents speak a special series of code words to him. From that moment on, David loves his parents deeply and without reserve. His parents return his love, and all is well until one day a cure for their real son's illness is found and he is revived. David's newly awakened "brother" resents David and torments him. The mother also comes to resent her artificial son. Taking a cue straight from The Wicked Stepmother's Handbook, she drives David out into the woods in the family's futuristic, three-wheeled car, then abandons him.

The mother is typical of the human characters in A.I. They are all portrayed as insensitive, selfish, or just plain cruel. Only the robots seem to care for one another. (In the short story on which A.I. is based, "Super-Toys Last All Summer Long" by Brian Aldiss, the mother struggles with her decision to return David to the factory where he was made.)

In the movie, David wanders through the forest with only his robotic toy Teddy for company. He is befriended by another robot, who helps him in his quest to become a real boy. If only he can become real, David believes his mother will love him again.

But an accident traps David at the bottom of the ocean. There he stays for thousands of years—long after his power supply is exhausted. By this time an ice age has left the Earth a frozen wasteland inhabited by an advanced race of robots. Human civilization has passed away—whether destroyed or absorbed by the robots, we are never told.

The robots revive David and grant him his wish: one last day with his mother.

could communicate with one another through infrared beams, teaching each other phrases and songs. If one of them began laughing, all other Furbys within earshot would soon be laughing too. The few people ever to report this phenomenon described the effect as chilling. Said one witness, "It was as if they were all in on some joke."

At $30 each, the Furbys were poised for global domination. Their plan collapsed when, just two short years after they triggered their first Christmas rampages in 1998, their popularity mysteriously dissipated.

Some Assembly Required

So maybe you're not up to raiding the junkyard or even the local hardware store to construct your own robot, but at the same time you know those off-the-shelf toys aren't going to amuse you for long. For you, there are robotic kits—toys with some assembly required. The simplest snap together in a few minutes to make a cart that will start or stop at the sound of a handclap. The most sophisticated require the use of screwdrivers and soldering irons for assembly and may consist of hundreds of parts. The latter are not for the technologically shy, but assuming you have none of those pesky leftover pieces when you're all done, you'll have a real working robot.

The Lynx 6 robotic arm can grasp just about anything within its reach up to the size of a spool of thread. Its motions are controlled through a home computer reading program you either write yourself or download from Lynxmotion's website.

Depending on exactly what you add to it, the arm can perform a variety of tasks. For example, with the aid of a small videocamera and the right programming it could sort through a row of colored balls, select only the blue ones, and drop them into a cup.

Among the most mesmerizing kit robots are the Hexapods—walking, six-legged bugs. There's something about the fluid, precise movements of these toys that puts them in a different class from even the most advanced off-the-shelf robots. Scientific institutions such as Carnegie Mellon, MIT, and NASA use these kits for their own research projects.

For the privilege of blistering your fingers with a soldering iron and picking through the carpet in search of dropped pieces, you can pay as much as $800. Still, if you're wondering if you're suited to a career in robotics or artificial intelligence, this could be a valuable first step to finding out.

Two Lynx 6 robotic arms battle it out on the checkerboard. Depending on the skills of the hobbyists who built these robots, they could be controlled either directly by human operators or by a checkers-playing program running on a home computer.

Robosapien

If your mechanical abilities are taxed by instructions like "Insert two AA batteries," something that comes out of the box in one piece might be a better choice.

Robosapien is a burly mechanical man standing about 30 centimeters (1 foot) tall on a pair of blocky feet that resemble bumper cars. The feet have to be big because each holds two D batteries. These are the power source for Robosapien's seven motors, and by concentrating the heaviest part of the machine in the feet, they help keep the robot from tipping over when it walks.

Robosapien waddles along by rocking its torso from side to side. When it steps forward with its left foot, it leans right, and vice versa. This helps its feet to clear the ground as it advances with its rather awkward gait. It's no ASIMO, but it does know how to hold an audience. The first thing it does upon awakening is stretch and yawn. It acknowledges most other commands with a belch. When put to sleep again, it snores in a manner reminiscent of Curly of the Three Stooges.

In addition to walking forward or backward, the robot can deliver a karate chop, turn, grasp objects, burp, whistle, dance, and even throw a small plastic bucket that comes with it. Its eyes glow and it speaks—well, growls is probably more accurate. The only words

101

Robosapien actually says are "ouch" if certain of its fingertips are touched and "Rosebud"—which it murmurs just before powering down.

Robosapien caught the attention of consumers and the toy industry partly because of its intimidating appearance and partly because it can be ordered to perform its 67 different actions in any sequence. In effect, it's programmable. The beauty is, you don't have to learn a programming language to operate it. It's really no more difficult than programming a sequence of songs into your CD player. And it's done in much the same way—by pressing buttons on a remote control.

The man who designed Robosapien is Mark Tilden, a Canadian physicist who has worked at Los Alamos, the high-energy weapons laboratory in New Mexico, and subscribes to the bottom-up theory of AI. The resemblance between Tilden, with his broad shoulders and booming voice, and his invention is not lost on most of the people who meet the man in person. In fact, all of Robosapien's vocalizations were digitized from a recording of Tilden's voice.

Tilden's strategy in designing Robosapien was to appeal to a generation raised on video games. He reasoned that these people— used to spending large amounts of money on their toys—might be lured out of virtual reality and

Robosapien is billed as "the first affordable humanoid robot." Operated by remote control, it has numerous functions, including the ability to walk, turn, and pick up items.

into the real world by the right product. He was right. WowWee, the company that manufactures Robosapien, sold millions of them over the Christmas season in 2004.

Although Robosapien is expensive by toy standards, with a retail price of roughly $100 US, previous robots with anywhere near the same capabilities cost several times as much. Tilden kept costs down by designing the prototype using analog circuitry that employs just a few transistors—considered primitive technology by modern designers.

Eventually, technicians had to design digital equivalents before they could begin mass production of the toy, but Tilden's economical design cut costs during the crucial first phase of the project.

Robosapien is a long way from Hasbro's Walkie Talkie, but apart from switches on three of its fingers and a microphone, it has no ability to sense or react to its environment, and answers only to its remote control. However, its ability to store and carry out a series of commands does make it a true robot.

How Much Is That Doggie in the Window?

Probably more than you have. Convinced that what their customers really want is a substitute pet, the Sony Corporation unleashed its top-of-the-line entertainment robot upon the world in the form of a mechanical dog called AIBO in 1999. At that time there were only about 5,000 available, and they were snapped up by consumers despite their $2,500 US price tags.

AIBO was the size of a very stocky chihuahua—although it probably weighed more—and was a sophisticated robot even by today's standards. The idea was to create a robotic puppy with some rudimentary ability to interact with its environment, learn from its experiences, and alter its own programming over time. Each AIBO would develop differently according to its environment and, in particular, how its owner responded to it.

It came out of the box with a number of behaviors already programmed into it. It could sit, offer a paw for shaking, make R2-D2–like noises, and even get back onto its paws if knocked over. It could play with its very own pink ball. The owner's manual encouraged people to stroke the dog on its back, its chin, or the top of its head to activate pressure sensors. In response, LEDs on AIBO's body would flash, signaling pleasure. Over time, AIBO would exhibit the rewarded behaviors more often, just as a live dog responds to affection. It would also perform its tricks in response to the right voice commands, and display a range of "emotions" through its posture and light displays.

So how good was AIBO as a substitute pet? The answer depended on the owner. Some quickly grew tired of its limited number of behaviors. They found that it walked and responded too slowly, and were disappointed with the musical sounds it made; they wanted to hear more doglike noises—growling or barking. They also found the dog's many motors too noisy—so noisy that AIBO couldn't hear voice commands when it was moving. AIBO *was* able to hear its command words when it was docked in its charging station. If these words come up in a conversation going on in the same room, it made a pinging sound. This annoyed many owners—particularly the ones who found it difficult to get the dog to respond to voice commands when it was supposedly up and alert.

In short, people comparing AIBO to a real dog were disappointed. Curiously, though, none of them claimed to miss paper-training their AIBO or having it come home reeking of skunk. On the other hand, those who compared it to, say, a Furby were pleased with their purchase. AIBO had temperature,

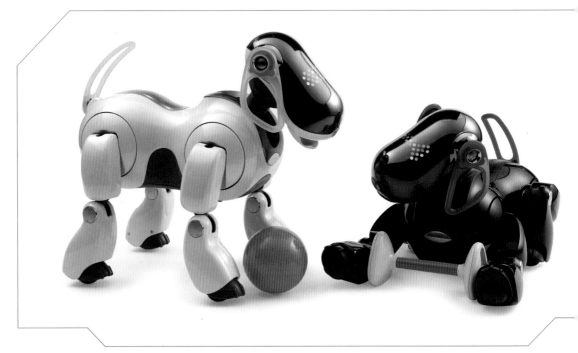

infrared, and vibration sensors and 20 movable joints. It could avoid walking off ledges and—with less success—running into objects. These owners were charmed by many of its programmed actions as well, such as getting up and shaking its head after falling over.

Since the introduction of the prototype, several models have come and gone. The latest goes by the affectionate name of AIBO ERS-7M2. It has a primitive camera in its nose and can recognize its owner. It can also communicate with a home computer through a wireless link and report the arrival of e-mails or upload pictures of its surroundings. Optional cards inserted in its back allow you to change its programming. Its hearing and vision are improved, and it can now find its own way back to its charging station when the batteries get low. Word has it that it will attack a Bell and Howell Mailmobile on sight.

None of these features is likely to win over owners hoping for a real dog, but the much lower price tag—about $2,000 US—might make them less inclined to take it back to the store.

Toys Are Us

Unlike other robots, the value of a toy robot is not measured by how much work it saves someone. Packbot and *Voyager* have jobs to do, but our toys have only to amuse us. And so it is worth reflecting on our choice in amusements. Do we gape at a six-story monster crushing an automobile in its jaws? Or would we rather cuddle a doll that coos at our touch? Or build an arm whose only purpose is to obey our instructions to the millimeter? Our toys say much about us.

Every Sony AIBO comes with its own ball and bone, and can perform a variety of tricks with them. The robots recognize their toys with videocameras able to key on the distinctive pink color of the accessories.

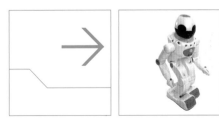

chapter 7
The Future

"We are on the edge of a robot revolution." Roboticists have been saying this for about 40 years. It's a bit like getting up each morning and declaring, "It will rain tomorrow." Sooner or later you will be right. There are few scientists who don't believe that eventually robots will be a part of our everyday lives. The question is, will the revolution start tomorrow? Or has it already begun?

Unless you work in a factory, your chances of bumping into a robot today are small—mainly because robots themselves keep bumping into things. As we noted earlier, robots just aren't ready for the real world. What will it take for robots to enter into our homes and lives?

Most people agree that the robot revolution is waiting for a good artificial brain. There's very little a robot couldn't do today if only it were smart enough. Some say that creating a humanlike brain is just a matter of matching the human brain's processing, or computing, ability. At present, the processing power for a microchip of a given size doubles about every 18 months. That's because with improvements in a process known as optical lithography, the number of switches that can be etched on a microchip of a given size doubles every 18 months.

This regular doubling of processing capacity is known as Moore's Law. If it continues at this rate (and some say we won't be able to continue for more than another 15 years), we'll have a home computer with the processing power of the human brain in another 25 years or so.

But will a computer that has the processing power of a human brain be as intelligent as a human being? That depends on whether we can write the software to take advantage of all that processing power. We still don't understand the software that operates our own brains.

In the meantime, how will robots develop and change our world?

The Near Future

Hans Moravec is the principal research scientist at the Carnegie Mellon University Robotics Institute. In late 1997 he predicted that the first mass-produced robots that are *not* toys would be available for purchase "within the next 5 to 10 years…" Moravec used the example of a robotic vacuum cleaner, and predicted that it would have enough intelligence to recognize furniture, map out a room, and cover the whole floor without vacuuming the same spot too many times.

He was partly right about the vacuum cleaner. The latest models do have the ability to avoid stairs, detect particularly dirty patches and run over them repeatedly, as well as find their way back to a charging station when their batteries run low. But none of these machines is actually visualizing a room in the way Moravec had predicted. A robovac with a basic ability to "see" a room might make it to market soon, but it seems doubtful with the more primitive models already selling well.

The next major change is likely to be the introduction of robotic vehicles—that is, vehicles that navigate without human pilots or drivers. Airliners already take off and land in bad weather under computer control. The only thing preventing commercial robotic flight at present is the public's acceptance of flying without a human pilot. And who can blame us? Most of us can live with rebooting the home computer when it hangs now and then; the same might not be true of a computer flying an airplane. But in truth, modern commercial jets already depend entirely on computers to fly.

A commercial airline will probably sell tickets for its first pilotless flight sometime around the year 2015. The savings realized in pilot wages and flight scheduling will cause all the

Although this science-fiction thriller is set less than 15 years in the future, the robots in it (called replicants) resemble people so closely that it takes an elaborate psychological test to tell them apart. The replicants work mainly in colonies in outer space—presumably somewhere in our solar system. It seems unlikely now that we can develop such advanced robots by 2019, but of course in 1982, when the movie was made, that future was a lot further away.

Blade Runner tells the story of Rick Deckard, a man who has to find and kill four replicants who have returned to Earth from their jobs "off world." The replicants are looking for the man who designed them. They have been built with a very short lifespan (four years) and hope to find a way to extend their lives. Because they have developed a strong will to survive, the replicants are angry at having been created with a built-in expiry date. They kill several people in their search.

Hunting down the replicants is not easy for Deckard because they are much faster and stronger then human beings, and he soon finds the tables turned: one of the replicants is hunting *him!*

The film never tries to explain the technologies that make the replicants possible. It simply shows them to us and asks the question, "If we could create these beings, what might they do?" At first the replicants are presented as being evil, but in the end they are only seeking answers to the same questions that people are: "Who made us, and for what purpose?" and "What should we do with our very short lives?"

other airlines to quickly follow suit. It will also become virtually impossible to hijack an airplane because the computers controlling them will be protected inside vaultlike enclosures.

Today, advances in self-driving vehicles are confined to avoiding accidents and handling emergencies. There are now cars that use radar to brake if they get too close to other objects. But if we are already turning over a car's controls to computers during emergencies, will it be long before cars control their own operation for the entire journey? Robotic cars will probably be practical within another 12 years, and available at about the same time as the first airliners fly without pilots.

But will automakers be willing to build such a car? Once they do, they will have to assume the blame for any accidents their products are involved in. Also, a lot of people *like* driving. Still, there will come a time when robotic cars are clearly safer than those driven by people. Insurance costs for people in robotic cars will drop, a strong incentive for everyone to leave the driving to their vehicles.

Self-driven vehicles could lead to advances in other areas too, such as law enforcement. A robotic police car equipped with cameras might roam the streets, sending pictures to a dispatcher. When a crime is witnessed, it could automatically call a manned patrol car to the location. Such a vehicle might also offer a refuge to someone being assaulted or threatened until police arrive. Just knowing their crimes were being recorded would deter many criminals.

Fully automated crime-fighting will have to wait for major advances like mechanical arms with the strength to wrestle a cuffed suspect into the back seat of a patrol car but with the dexterity to do it without banging his head on the door frame—a skill police officers acquire only through years of practice.

Universal Robots—the Revolution Arrives

According to Moravec, the first generation of universal robots—machines with hands and arms able to do a variety of household chores—should be available by the year 2020. That's earlier than many experts in the field of robotics would predict. Still, most agree that somewhere between the years 2029 and 2035 a robot able to wash, cook, and clean will become a reality. These machines will execute a variety of programs while taking into account their surroundings with some sort of robotic vision. They will be able to recognize common objects.

These robots could act as care aides, assisting the physically disabled. They could understand and follow spoken instructions, such as "Pick up that fork" or "Help me out of this chair." In a restaurant (or at home) such a robot could follow a recipe and cook a meal or bring it to your table. It might even be able to recognize faces and remember who ordered what.

By the time the first universal robots are introduced, most manufacturing will already be done by robots, so there will be very few human factory workers left to replace. Instead, the robots will begin taking the jobs of the tens of millions of workers in the service sector.

The service sector is made up of tasks that require the presence of a human being. These are jobs like cook, cashier, gardener, and flight attendant. Their duties cannot be carried out by a person in another country because shipping a burger and fries from overseas isn't practical no matter how much cheaper labor is there—at least not yet.

Already, in North America, more people work in service jobs than in any other type of employment besides government jobs. If these

In this chilling science-fiction story, the end of the world as we know it begins in a fast-food restaurant in the year 2010. It starts innocently enough. To ensure that service is equally good in all of its locations, the Burger-G chain installs a personal computer running a program called Manna in each of its thousand outlets.

Every employee is issued a set of headphones. Manna instructs the employees using voice commands such as "Jane, please close your register. Then we will clean the women's rest-room." Jane responds by saying "Okay," closing her till, and heading towards the ladies' room.

Manna knows when Jane has entered the bathroom because it uses the headsets to track the movements of all the store's employees. It instructs Jane in each step of the cleaning process. "Place the 'wet floor' warning cone outside the door please," it orders her.

"Okay," answers Jane.

Manna knows when the bathrooms need cleaning and the garbage cans need emptying because it monitors customer volumes through the tills. It times all of the employees at their

people are replaced by robotic workers, unemployment will soar. Some predict economic disaster. Without workers to pay into retirement funds, the main source of income for the elderly will collapse. Unable to pay their mortgages, the unemployed will lose their homes as banks foreclose on them. Although the prices of

manufactured goods will fall, few will earn enough money to buy them.

Because robots will be able to manufacture everything so cheaply, only land and raw materials will hold their value. Robot farming will lower food prices a little, but because land will still be essential for agriculture, food will be worth tasks and urges them to hurry up if they take too long. It tells them when to start and end their breaks.

The least efficient workers are soon fired. The remaining employees no longer have to think about what they're doing. In effect, they become human robots.

Efficiency in the Burger-G chain rises. Soon its competitors adopt the system. Then other major chains—home electronics stores, building supply outlets, supermarkets—purchase their own versions of Manna. Airports and government services follow.

Then, in the year 2023, a breakthrough in robotic vision makes general-purpose robots practical, and real robots begin replacing even the most efficient human employees. The millions of

unemployed are soon unable to pay their rents or mortgages. They are moved to enormous government housing projects. There, they sleep in dormitories and are fed in cafeterias. They are kept apart from the small percentage of the population that has grown rich.

"Manna" is a fascinating look at two pressing problems in modern North America: the uncontrolled march of technology and the concentration of wealth in our society. Most of the story could happen tomorrow, without any further technological advances.

"Manna" was written by Marshall Brain, the inventor of the famous How Stuff Works website. The complete story can be found at www.marshallbrain.com.

more than manufactured goods.

The following generations of robots will be even more intelligent. By about 2040 they will be as reliable as skilled human workers, perhaps more so. At this point even highly trained workers will start to lose their jobs. Robots will do the work of surgeons, engineers, and technicians.

Of course, this is only one scenario. Some experts—for example Helen Greiner, chairman of the iRobot corporation—think that a robot exceeding human abilities is closer to 100 years away. Others believe that when universal robots are first developed, they will be so expensive that they will only replace a few human workers. Then, as the price of robots falls, they will slowly infiltrate the workforce. We will have time to adjust to the changes brought to our economy.

But what if Dr. Moravec is right? What if, starting in the year 2020, the first universal robots begin to appear in our homes and offices? It's reasonable to assume that within 10 years of their arrival they will start doing our most tedious and unfulfilling jobs.

After all, this is exactly what we have always hoped robots would do. But what will the people who once did these jobs do? Won't many of them find jobs in the growing robotics industry?

The answer is no, at least not in North America. And any robots built here would probably be built by other robots.

If our current economic system does not change, the people who own or supply the companies that manufacture the robots will become even richer, and the people whose jobs they take will be left with nothing.

The real challenge of the robot revolution is not just inventing these machines, but finding a way of giving everyone a share of the wealth they will reap.

The robot revolution can be the fulfillment of a long-awaited dream or it can be a nightmare. It depends on how well we plan over the next few years, before the robot revolution overtakes us.

After the Revolution

Suppose that, 45 years from now, we have acted wisely. Robots now do all our work for us. They serve us in restaurants, mow our lawns, drive us from place to place. Students still go to school, but they get to learn more about really cool stuff they're interested in and less about stuff they *have* to know. After all, you won't have to worry about getting a job when you graduate. That's because at the end of each month you'll receive a check from the government funded largely by the robotics tax. It's enough to buy food and most of the manufactured goods you could ever desire.

After graduation you'll have all the time you want to play your

In *The Terminator*, a robot from the future is cloaked in living flesh to allow it to travel through time and also make it a little less conspicuous during its murderous rampage once it arrives in 1984. At the film's climax, the outer, living part of the robot is burned away in a car crash, revealing the mechanisms within.

In this action film, a robot known as the Terminator is sent from a future dominated by malevolent machines to kill Sara Conner. Sara is the Terminator's target because she will one day give birth to John Conner, a man who will lead the human resistance against the machines. The machines reason that if they can kill the mother, the son will never be born.

Outwardly, the Terminator looks like a human being. This is because only living creatures can be sent through time, and so the robot must be cloaked in human flesh. (The real reason is that the producers did not have the budget to create a convincing robot for the entire length of the movie. It was cheaper to have an actor play the part.)

In the sequel *Terminator 2: Judgment Day* (1991), the machines, having failed to kill Sara Conner,

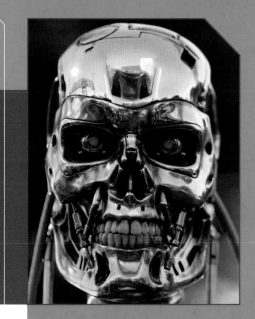

send a second robot into the past, this time to kill John Conner as a boy. This second robot, the T1000, is a far more advanced model made of a single blob of liquid metal controlled by forces that are never explained. The T1000 can shape itself into almost anything. It can look like a person, a vending machine—any object roughly the size of an adult human being. If it is splattered into pieces, it can reassemble itself.

As the T1000 arrives in our time, the human resistance fighters from the future send back an original-model Terminator to protect John Conner. This original Terminator gradually develops feelings for John and his mother as it battles to save them from the T1000.

The Terminator movies employ two ideas that show up again and again in almost every story about robots. The first is that our inventions will try to destroy us. The second is that robots are so intrigued with human emotions that they eventually long to experience feelings themselves. Curiosity and emotions evolved in animals as aids to our survival. Although they would probably not be necessary for a robot's well-being, emotional responses might be included in a robot's programming so that people could more easily interact with it.

The cold, relentless pursuit of the original Terminator was what gave the story its nightmarish quality, and part of what made the film a hit.

antique PlayStation games, but that will be pretty tame compared with going down to the local Roborange, where you get to stalk through the stone corridors of a robot-built castle, blasting away at your robotic opponents with a handheld particle weapon.

So now that robots finally walk among us, there are two important questions to consider. The first is, how will we treat these machines? We know how we treat them today. We get them to weld the same parts together over and over again on an assembly line, or walk into active volcanoes, or clean up after nuclear accidents. There's nothing wrong with giving such jobs to machines. It's safe to say that if the robot explorer *Spirit* is successfully taking a soil sample on the surface of Mars or scattered in a thousand pieces at the bottom of an impact crater, it makes no difference to *Spirit*.

But what if, someday, we build robots that become self-aware, or conscious, once they're switched on?

You and I are self-aware. In addition to whatever you are concentrating on, whether it's getting to school on time or the fact that your elbow hurts, there is another layer of your mind that stands back from what you're doing and observes. You tend to think of this part as the real you. It's your personality, the part of your mind that plans and has desires and feelings about all that goes on around you.

If you're really absorbed in something you're doing—playing a sport or listening to a great song—you pretty much forget about this part of yourself. You're "in the moment." It's when things are going badly that you're *really* self-aware. Like when you're in the middle of an oral presentation to the class and you suddenly think, "Did I put on any pants this morning?"

Will robots and computers someday be self-aware? Many people say no. They believe that consciousness is something special to living creatures. The problem is, you can't really prove that you're self-aware. No one else can hear that little voice in your head commenting on what you see and do. Proving that machines are self-aware will be just as impossible.

We wouldn't think of forcing a person to do a job they don't want to do. Okay, we would think of it, but it's now generally agreed that doing so is wrong. The accepted procedure is to offer workers something in return for their efforts—usually money. Forcing people to work without giving them some kind of payment is slavery.

So what do we do if we build robots that claim they are self-aware? Once an intelligent, conscious being is created, does it matter whether it was born or assembled? Is it right to force it to do only what we want it to? Or should we give it the same rights as people have? Will we just ask the robots to work for us and offer to pay them? There goes the free labor!

The Differential Analyzer was an entirely mechanical computer built at MIT in the early 1930s. The positions of different rods within the machine represented numerical values, and calculations were made through the movements of the rods as well as the cams and gears connecting them. Depending on the equations being solved, the mechanism would have to be rearranged. One of the machine's inventors, Vannevar Bush, looks on.

115

If the first question we must ask ourselves is, How will we treat conscious machines? the second question is even more troubling: How will they treat us?

You might think that it doesn't really matter; we will control these robots through careful programming, employing rules such as Isaac Asimov's three laws of robotics. But most people agree that if we ever do create machines as intelligent as ourselves, within a very short time we will be creating machines much, much smarter than we are. This is because artificial intelligence has several advantages over human intelligence.

For one, machine evolution progresses at a much faster rate than biological evolution. A human generation is about 25 years. That's the time it takes for human beings to mature and have children. The shorter a species' generation time, the faster it evolves. That's why bacteria can develop immunities to drugs in just a few years—their generations are often only minutes or hours.

Computers don't reproduce, but they do evolve over time. If we consider each new model of computer to be a generation, then their generation time is several months, or at most a year, which is how often new models are introduced.

Not only is a computer's generation time much shorter than ours, but each new generation is an improvement over the last. Computers have steadily been getting faster and smaller because engineers deliberately design them that way. In contrast, human beings and other species must wait for chance mutations in their DNA to improve their bodies. Despite the huge number of people in the world, such mutations are very rare, and most either make no difference to our bodies or actually damage them.

For these reasons, *Mecha sapiens*, if invented, will evolve much more quickly than *Homo sapiens* ever did.

Another great advantage machines will have over humans is that electronic memory and processing are much faster than human thinking. Right now we have the advantage of having millions of times more switches (called neurons) in our brains than the fastest computers have in theirs. What our neurons lack in speed, we make up for in numbers. But within another 20 years or so, if Moore's Law holds, we will lose the numbers advantage. We will build computers that have more switches than our brains do, and each of those switches will be

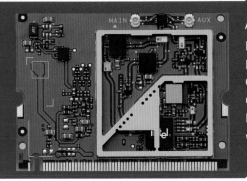

As the number of transistors that engineers can pack into a given area has grown, their average price has shrunk. In 1968, a single transistor cost roughly a dollar. Today, an integrated circuit, or chip, on a board like this one may contain hundreds of thousands of transistors. Each is worth less than .00001 *cents*.

millions of times faster than ours.

Finally, computers have perfect memory. Unless they're damaged, they don't forget anything. Also, their knowledge can be transferred from one to another without loss.

So, within about 20 years computer brains will have greater capacity and greater speed than the human brain, perfect memory, and access to any knowledge possessed by any other computer. Of course, before any of this can happen, we still have to invent software that will allow computers to actually *think*. Right now, we have no idea of how to do that. We may never. But if we figure it out, even if we build something like Asimov's three laws into their programming, they might easily think their way around such rules.

Cosmists vs. Terrans

Hugo de Garis is one of the world's leading experts in artificial intelligence. He believes that as we come closer to building these super-intelligent brains, the world will divide into two groups. One group will be the Cosmists, who believe we should continue to develop artificial intellects, or Artilects as he calls them. The other group will be the Terrans—the people who think we should not. He believes that the Terrans will try to stop the Cosmists from building an Artilect smarter than a human by waging a war in which billions of us will die.

If the Cosmists do succeed in inventing an Artilect, what will it think of us? No one knows. It might have a special fondness for the human beings who gave birth to it, just as we have a special fondness for our parents. Or it may not think about us at all, and brush us aside as we would a fly.

Despite what he believes is a very real danger, de Garis continues to work on building an artificial brain.

117

Other experts in the field of artificial intelligence believe Hugo de Garis greatly exaggerates the danger that Artilects pose to us. Ray Kurzweil is an author who writes about artificial intelligence and has created software able to translate spoken words into text and vice versa. Like de Garis, Kurzweil believes that we will one day design super-intelligent robots. But he also believes that, by that time, human beings will be just as smart. He predicts that as artificial memory and processing power grow in capacity, we will gradually incorporate these advances into our own brains. We will start by implanting tiny chips to enhance our memory or allow us to communicate directly with computers. We will replace diseased or damaged organs and limbs with mechanical ones and become cyborgs.

Later, we will discover how it is that the cells in our brains generate thoughts. When our bodies grow old and die, our minds will be transferred entirely to computers that control robotic bodies. These bodies will never age or suffer pain or infection. Instead of becoming enemies or nuisances to the robots,

we will *be* the robots. Once again, this would depend on another invention that we can now only imagine: we will have to find a way of connecting artificial chips to our nerves and brain cells.

If we are ever able to do this, the world and the way we see it will change dramatically. Arthur C. Clarke, a science-fiction writer and astronomer, also predicts that we will one day merge our bodies with machines, at first to cure disease and postpone death, but ultimately for the pleasure of it.

If a bee stings you on the hand, you're unaware that the pain is really taking place in your brain, an arm's length away. You just think, "My hand hurts." Future technology might allow us to extend the reach of our senses well beyond an arm's length—to kilometers or hundreds of kilometers. While our bodies, or perhaps only our brains, remain safe and protected in some central place, our senses will range over the whole Earth—from the stratosphere to the bottom of the ocean. With the right connections to advanced robots, we could experience these explorations as if we were actually traveling.

Nanobots

The robot revolution depends mainly on development of artificial intelligence, but there are other areas of robotic research that could bring even greater changes.

Right now, the usual way of making almost anything is to take a larger piece of some material, whether it is wood or metal or glass, and use tools to shape it into a useful object—usually by removing some of the original material. For example, to make a baseball bat, we cut down a tree. Then we remove the branches to leave a log. We saw the log into blocks of wood. Then we take one of the blocks, put it on a lathe, and shave away wood until

we have a bat. As Richard Feynman (the physicist who invented the concept of nanotechnology) put it, we work from the top down. But what if we were to work the other way? What if we were to take the smallest bits of a material—molecules or atoms—and build the objects we need from the bottom up?

In this artist's concept, a pair of nanobots—microscopically small robots—use laser beams to destroy a virus within a human lung cell. At present, such machines are strictly fantasy, as no one has any practical idea of how they might be made.

119

At first this seems a ridiculous notion. After all, even a pretty small object—for example, a pen—has trillions of atoms in it. Making a pen an atom at a time would take forever! But what if you were trying to make something *really* tiny—something so small that it had only a few thousands or millions of molecules in it?

That's the theory behind *nano-technology*. The word *nano* is from the Greek word for "dwarf."

Gray goo is the imaginary substance that would result if self-replicating nanobots (or *nanites*, as they are sometimes called) were to multiply out of control. To reproduce, the tiny robots would consume and rearrange the molecules in whatever raw materials they could find. Eventually, everything would be turned into a soup of nanites covering the Earth.

→

Nanotechnology is the science of fabricating tiny machines. The advantage of building from the bottom up is that you can work with great precision. In theory, if we could make robots tiny enough, we could use them to control things that happen on a molecular scale, like the processes inside the cells of our bodies or on the surfaces of computer chips.

But how do you go about fastening individual atoms to one another? In fact, getting them to stick together isn't a problem at all; many atoms just combine naturally when you place two of them close enough to each other. Living things do this all the time. They use protein molecules to assemble other molecules in order to make bone, muscle, and blood. It's how our bodies grow and heal.

REMEMBER

ONLY YOU
CAN PREVENT GRAY GOO

NEVER RELEASE NANOBOT ASSEMBLERS
WITHOUT REPLICATION LIMITING CODE

www.anigami.com

Artificial nanomachines would also gather and manipulate individual molecules, but instead of proteins, they would likely be made of metals or carbon. They would, in effect, be tiny robots. Nanobots.

Scientists today have only succeeded in making a few simple machines on the nano-scale: gears, axles, levers. But in theory, nanobots could be highly complex. They could float in our bloodstreams, repairing diseased cells before they reproduce, or fill dental cavities with incredible precision, or cure nearsightedness by changing the shape of the lens of the eye.

If you had enough nanobots all working at one task, they could be used to fabricate objects on an everyday scale. Nanobots could replace factories, assembling even quite large objects from the bottom up. Nanobots are far too small to see, so the things they make would appear to just form themselves out of rock or soil or air—whatever the source material was. There would be no assembly line, no factory.

Theoretically, sophisticated nanobots would give mankind nearly complete control over the material world. Anything we can conceive of could be built almost instantly, in place, out of the raw materials of Earth.

But the ultimate technology poses the ultimate threat. The only way to produce the trillions of nano-bots necessary to do these amazing things would be to have them make copies of themselves. But suppose that something went wrong with such a robot's programming and it didn't know when to stop? The nanobots would just keep making copies of themselves until they ran out of raw material. They could consume the whole Earth down to the molten mantle! This is some-times called the "gray goo" problem, as it is believed that a bunch of uncontrolled nanobots would resemble a grayish, gooey substance.

Can We Live with Second Place?

In the science-fiction film *I, Robot*, the main character—a police detective who despises and fears the humanoid robots that have become commonplace—interrogates a robot suspected of murder. He asks it, "Can a robot cure cancer or compose a symphony?"

In return, the robot asks, "Can you?"

The detective in *I, Robot* is trying desperately to maintain his belief that human beings are superior. As a species, we take pride in our intelligence and ability to create. These are the things we do better than any other animal. But what if we lose that special place in the world to robots? What will be the point of doing anything if we know that machines can do it better?

There are many scientists—including Hugo de Garis and Marshall Brain—who truly believe that robots will play a large part in our destiny as a species. Arthur C. Clarke has a different view: he believes just the opposite—that it is we who are a part of the robots' destiny. Perhaps it is different elsewhere, but here on Earth intelligence

evolved from life. It developed further with the use of tools. Gradually, the tools have grown more and more sophisticated, to the point where they may soon become intelligent themselves.

This pattern may be a very rare occurrence in the universe; we won't know until we are able to explore many other planets—by either traveling to them or contacting other intelligent beings. But there is also a chance that this is the normal course of events in the evolution of intelligence—machine intelligence.

Clarke believes our bodies will one day be merged with machines, but he does not believe the cyborg partnership will last for long. Flesh and blood are simply too frail and will only be a hindrance to our freedom. Ultimately we will discard them, and machines will be the final vessels for our knowledge, our experience, and our individual beings.

If that is the case, then Clarke believes extinction of our species as we know it is nothing to fear; human beings will have served a noble purpose—acting as a bridge between animal life and the robots that will follow us.

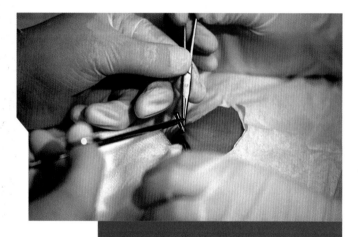

In 1998, professor of cybernetics Kevin Warwick had surgeons implant a silicon chip in his forearm. The chip allowed computers to track Warwick's movements within the building where he works. Warwick calls himself the world's first cyborg, but by any practical definition of the word, the first person to have a pacemaker implanted beat him to the title by 40 years.

Index

Photo credits